RIVERSIDE COMMUNITY COLLEGE
1916

P9-DUJ-969

ARE YOU RUNNING WITH ME, JESUS?

MALCOLM BOYD

ARE YOU RUNNING WITH ME, JESUS?

A SPIRITUAL COMPANION FOR THE 1990s

BEACON PRESS • BOSTON

Beacon Press
25 Beacon Street
Boston, Massachusetts 02108-2800

Beacon Press books
are published under the auspices of
the Unitarian Universalist Association of Congregations.

Printed in the United States of America

97 96 95 94 93 92 91 90 1 2 3 4 5 6 7 8

Text design by Lisa Diercks

Library of Congress Cataloging-in-Publication Data
Boyd, Malcolm.
Are you running with me Jesus? : a spiritual companion for the 1990s /
Malcolm Boyd.
p. cm.
ISBN 0-8070-7700-3
1. Prayer-books. I. Title.
BV245.B629 1990
242'.8—dc20 89-46063

To

Beatrice Boyd

Paul Roberts

Mary E. Lowe

Richard Allyn English

Virginia King

Paul Moore, Jr.

and

Mark Thompson

CONTENTS

ACKNOWLEDGMENTS

My deep gratitude is expressed to William Robert Miller and Joseph Cunneen, editors of the original edition; Thomas Fischer, my editor at Beacon Press; Ned Leavitt and Irene Webb of the William Morris Agency, who have charted the book's course with loving energy; St. Augustine by-the-Sea Episcopal Church in Santa Monica, California, for letting me be its writer-priest-in-residence and creating a nurturing environment in which I could write and grow—with special thanks to Fred Fenton and Elizabeth Habecker for true comradeship, honest criticism, and strong support; Marni Schneider, for sharing the inner journey; M. R. Ritley, who used her expertise with computerized composition systems to prepare the manuscript for publication; and the countless people who have communicated to me in various ways how *Are You Running with Me, Jesus?* has touched their lives.

INTRODUCTION

Twenty-five years ago a book of eighty-nine short prayers and meditations I wrote was published. Langston Hughes called them, simply, poems. The most unexpected event of my life up to that time, and certainly one of the most exhilarating, was when *Are You Running with Me, Jesus?* deeply touched the lives of people and was critically acclaimed.

However, the book emerged in silence, with virtually no reviews. Although *Time* printed three of the writings, it made no comment. Five months after publication the *New York Times* ran a major review praising the book. Twelve months after publication *Are You Running with Me, Jesus?* was selling five thousand copies a week. The title became familiar in the press and on television and radio; an outpouring of affection for the book took the form of thousands of letters; its name began to appear on banners in peace demonstrations.

What had happened? The spirit of the times had a lot to do with the book's growing reception. There was excitement and a positive thrust in religion that could not be separated from a comparable secular mood, with its Peace Corps imagery of hope, the civil rights struggle, a strong public consciousness of a potential to effect significant changes in society, and a near-universal yearning for peace.

I wrote most of the book during the summer and fall of 1964 in Detroit, where I lived in the inner city. The meditation that begins, "Look up at that old window where the old guy is sitting," was based, for example, on a street scene just five blocks from my lodgings near Wayne State University, where I was a chaplain. "The old house is nearly all torn down, Jesus" was a view directly across the street. "The kids are smiling, Jesus, on the tenement stoop" was six blocks away. "In this ugly red building, old people are waiting for death" was three blocks away.

The impulse to write the book sprang from my increasing inability to pray. I had always assumed that prayer was necessarily verbal. I forced myself to use the archaic language of liturgical prayer, battling my growing disillusionment and boredom. Wasn't God supposed to be *up there?* When this neat system collapsed for me, I virtually stopped praying, except for using the Lord's Prayer.

In the spring of 1964 a group of Roman Catholic laity and clergy invited me to visit Israel and Rome with them. At one point in the trip we visited the island of Cyprus for a day or so; afterward we proceeded by ship to Haifa. On Cyprus the men lived dormitory-style in a hostel. One afternoon everybody was taking a nap, despite the sounds of distant gunfire being exchanged by Greek and Turkish Cypriots.

I lay on my cot, trying to pray. Then I picked up a ballpoint pen and a notebook. "It's morning, Jesus," I wrote, "and here's that light and sound all over again." The time of day was wrong, but I wasn't being literalistic.

That was the basis of the first entry in *Are You Running with Me, Jesus?* The book was begun. Of course, I didn't know it at the time. I had no idea of writing a book at all. I was grappling with prayer and meditation, trying to get started in a new way. After the tour I put my notes aside. But that summer I again started thinking about and writing my sacred thoughts.

I sent the book to an editor who was a friend of mine. The publisher for whom he worked accepted it, and the original contract formally titled the book *Prayers for a Post-Christian Era.* The editor explained we would have to move very carefully if I wished the book to be called *Are You Running with Me, Jesus?* The publisher was less than enthusiastic about that proposal. Finally, the editor won approval of my title—but only because the publisher thought the book was doomed to peak at a mere four thousand sales. Thus, what difference could it make *what* the book was called?

Those incredible letters I received from readers were the first indication something exciting was happening to *Are You Running with Me, Jesus?* The communications filled pages, dealt with complex matters, were moving. But one terse message remains my favorite: "My sister and I are too old to run with Jesus as we used to," a woman wrote. "Now we're only able to walk with him. Jesus has taken us over some rough terrain but he stayed with us. Old and weary though we are, we can say there is no other way. His hand is large and secure, isn't it?"

The avalanche of letters informed me also that my own life was about to change in ways unknown to me. "Your thoughts, your highs and lows, are familiar to us all," one early reader wrote. An image of the author was being created. I could only stand back and watch in sometime bewilderment, wonder, and dismay.

I seldom used structured words in my own prayers or meditations any more, except for those uttered in a conversation where God's presence, or need, was particularly strongly felt. Prayerful reflections, for me, used to stand as something separate from other parts of my life. *But I came to learn that real prayer or meditation is not so much talking to God as just sharing God's presence,* generally in the most ordinary of situations.

I also learned how to feel free to be completely myself with God. Now, in a given situation, knowing that God is with me—perhaps revealed in another person, or persons—I speak out of the deep trust and love that can spring only from a healthy, tried, and authentic freedom. When my ideas of prayer changed, I realized it would no longer be offered to God *up there,* but to God *here;* it was to be natural and real, not phony or contrived; it was not about *other* things—as a rationalized fantasy or escape—but *these* things, however unattractive, jarring, or even socially outcast they might sometimes appear to be.

Prayer is so much more than most people give it credit for. Beyond words, it can be voting, making love, just standing there, being angry, being quiet, cooking spaghetti sauce, marching in a peace demonstration, watering a garden, attending an office meeting, listening, lying on a sick bed, dancing, swimming, getting married, starting a new job, walking on a crowded street. Prayer can be filled with color and fun, vitality and pain, hopelessness and starting over again. I like to look out at life as I see it, and pray about it.

An exciting aspect of prayer, for me, is that the old patriarchy is dead. God is not, I discovered, a hierarchical, autocratic, macho "Lord" of a clublike "holy of holies," nor is God an impersonal machine computing sins in a celestial corporate office above the clouds. It came to me that God is loving, even vulnerable, in a terribly unsentimental and profound way, demonstrating the depth, complexity, and holy simplicity of an extraordinary relationship with people.

I came to realize many prayers and meditations are uttered or felt without prescribed forms of piety, sometimes in language imagery that censors might label as profane. If you listen, you can hear sacred thoughts and reflections in the novels, songs, plays, and films of a wide range of contemporary artists. Authentic prayer bridges the heretical gulf between the sacred and secular, the holy and profane. Of course, to hear some genuine prayers, verbal or nonverbal, you must sense what is *not* said.

We encounter anti-prayers when confronted by worshipers who deny in their actions outside a church building what they "pray" about inside. So, there is a hypocritical gulf between mouthing prayers about racial justice and then resolutely manipulating a white power structure to keep nonwhites in housing ghettos, gridlock unemployment, and interminable second- or third-class citizenship.

Prayer, I have learned, is more my response to God than a matter of my own initiative. I believe Jesus Christ prays *in* me as well as *for* me. But my response—like the Psalmist's—is sporadic, moody, now despairing, now joyful, corrupted by my self-interest and frequent desire to manipulate God's love. The widespread, often hidden, community that is open to the Spirit of God—ranging from Christians to Buddhists, Jews to adherents of New Age consciousness, Jungians to committed members of peace movements—incarnates prayer in its essential life. My own prayer is a part of this. But many times when I am caught up in egoism or self-pity, I forget.

I am as conscious of experiencing God *everywhere* in life as a medieval person residing in the shadow of Chartres might be, or an ancient tribal person living close to the realities of nature. My sacred thoughts, prayers, reflections, and meditations reflect this.

What strikes me is the mysterious reality of the book's acceptance by vast numbers of people in all strata of American life—seekers and atheists, the elderly and the young, nuns and housewives, Jews and Christians, students and business executives, the establishment and the counterculture. Amusingly, Hugh D. Auchincloss, the great financial and social figure, asked me one day: "Why don't you write any prayers for stockbrokers?" It seemed to me that the book did offer prayers for stockbrokers, but that it also communicated with, and about, the powerless. I hoped so.

Now, a quarter of a century has passed since the appearance of *Are You Running with Me, Jesus?* I am also that much older as a human being. Recently I celebrated not only my sixty-sixth birthday but also my thirty-fourth anniversary as an Episcopal priest. Doing so, I found myself looking back upon the significant spiritual turning points in my life.

In 1951 I left a Hollywood career to enter a theological seminary. In 1961 I moved into an intense, risky, no-holds-barred involvement in the U.S. civil rights movement as an activist. In 1965 *Are You Running with Me, Jesus?* became a phenomenon as well as a book. As a result, it was necessary for me to confront and assimilate celebrity, and learn how to survive it. In 1968 I withdrew into a reflective, carefully structured life at Yale in Calhoun College while I privately experienced a crisis of faith. A Humpty Dumpty part of me had fallen and broken into pieces; I was in a serious spiritual crisis. *What* did I actually believe? Could I rediscover it or find it anew? I sought peace, intellectual honesty, and spiritual renewal.

In 1970 I entered into an even deeper spiritual search. For the most part I cut myself off from other people, stayed close to nature in the countryside of Michigan, and was nurtured by the steady, slow turning of the seasons, with their witness to God's creation and stability. In 1976 I came out of one of my life's closets when I revealed that I am a gay man. I experienced a rebirth, a being "born again" that reverberated through my entire life with its sheer spiritual intensity. The reaffirmed love of God for me as a person created in God's image became overpowering. The love of Jesus Christ, who shared every aspect of his human life in the Incarnation and is my Redeemer, set me afire with new hope and joy. The companionship of the Holy Spirit is, I found, nurturing, intimate, a limitless source of strength, and a guide to personal well-being and social responsibility.

In 1980 I joined the staff of St. Augustine by-the-Sea Episcopal Church in Santa Monica, California, and have had many wonderful years there.

Imagine my dismay, then, to confront a Mount Everest of turning points that apparently still lay ahead. Although loaded down with accouterments of what the world chooses to call achievement, I had to face a most crucial question: *What is the purpose of the rest of my life?* I hated to admit it, but despite everything I had to be grateful for, I was aware I had come perilously close to not growing anymore. I felt my life was, in an utterly surprising way, becoming encased in cement. Or, to put it differently, I believed that I was being painted into an inexplicable corner.

A whole room's floor was freshly painted before my eyes. In fact, paint now slopped over my shoes as I stood, huddled in a corner's tiny space. I decided I must summon all my energy, taking the last chance to leap through an open door. I had to get in touch anew with my conscience and intuition, feelings and senses. My life required new growth. The Book of Common Prayer says quite eloquently, "Deliver us from the presumption of coming to this Table for solace only, and not for strength; for pardon only, and not for renewal." The moment had once again come for me to get deeply involved in the quest for Christ's strength and renewal.

The answer seemed to lie not in my exterior life, but in my *interior* life. I entered upon a long period of Jungian therapy rooted in dream analysis. My dreams? They comprise a wondrous inner journey. This trip is quite unlike a cruise through the Greek islands, a flight to Brazil, or a trek from Vancouver to Montreal. It is all interior stuff. My dream journal turned into a bulging volume.

This journey is my individuation process. Scenes shift. People come and go. I perceive fresh territories and face thorny dilemmas. In a Buddhist sense, I confront problems that can be dealt with now—or else may await me, again and again, in the future. In a Christian sense, I can claim a freely offered gift of "new life" in salvation and joy, experience ecstasy and meaning, involve myself in life and share it with others—or I can choose the hell of isolation, lovelessness, and turn my back upon spontaneity because I choose to remain "in control."

I find to my delight that I am not at all alone on my spiritual journey. Companions are legion. There is a present spiritual hunger and thirst in people that reflects an overwhelming human need. It is different from the mood of 1965 when *Are You Running with Me, Jesus?* first appeared. Now there is anxiety, and also hope, about the emergence of a new century. The year 2000 comes closer. An earlier innocence has been replaced by a hard awareness of impinging realities. It is understood that youthful, fresh idealism is not enough. One has to connect with information about many aspects of life, and respond pragmatically. Old answers and familiar approaches do not suffice for a good reason. There are altogether new questions and problems.

In our highly materialistic, consumer-oriented, success-motivated society, there is found a spiritual wilderness. Conventional churchianity—too timid to address controversial social issues, publicly asexual, reciting traditional norms by rote, and devoid of passionately committed spiritual leaders—is unable to meet the challenge. Growing numbers of people are asking how to gain the world without losing one's soul. Or how to live a good, full life that has a deeply spiritual core.

I was astounded when I attended a "New Age Spirituality" conference recently. Two thousand people crowded onto a suburban campus on a Saturday morning. It was clear they had left behind their ties to traditional religion. These women and men came from roots in Judaism, Catholicism, and Protestantism, but felt that their religious past now stood obdurately in the way of their wished-for spiritual growth and progress. They expressed considerable frustration and anger toward religious traditions that, in their view, were negative and harmful, and somehow belonged more to a distant Middle Ages than contemporary life.

Like the people at that conference, I have had to question virtually every aspect of faith. What do professed beliefs *mean,* and mean *to me?* The time has come to be completely honest about this. New challenges to traditional theology come from divergent sources, including feminist theology, liberation theology, process thought, postmodernism, gay/lesbian spirituality and theology, and creation-centered spirituality.

In my view, God's revelation is not locked inside, or restricted to, the pages of any book, including the Bible. The revelation of God is a continuing process in the world. I believe that no religious organization has a right to place its own perpetuation and power *over* the struggles and needs of people. The feminist movement has underscored the motif of liberation and attacked an entrenched and outmoded patriarchy.

However, the Jesus of *Are You Running with Me, Jesus?* is still the Jesus whom I continue to run with, know, and love. From my perspective, Jesus Christ is inclusive, loving, enabling, sharing, and the most radical source of creative energy. Jesus incarnates humanness, pure holiness, androgyny, humor, passion, sexuality, and a commitment to justice.

While Jesus is the same, our world is not. The deep changes I find in it are reflected in these pages of the twenty-fifth anniversary edition of *Are You Running with Me, Jesus?* For one thing, environmental issues have startlingly moved to the forefront of our consciousness and experience. Survival itself is at stake, along with our common health. Tragically, we have let racial justice lag behind minimal decency and the requirements of an honest conscience. Women's rights and gay/lesbian rights have taken immense strides, yet even when a war has been won, battles remain to be waged. And ever new wars hang in the balance. Politics remains a dismayingly paradoxical arena in which forces of public service contend with the most flagrant, abusive assertions of self-interest against the public good.

New prayers in the book reflect my focus on these matters. Language has changed, too; it is constantly in flux. Twenty-five years ago blacks were called Negroes by the media; gay men and lesbians were called homosexuals. But the most dramatic changes are found in the area of inclusive language. A quarter of a century ago "he" was used to describe persons of both genders as a universal kind of human description; God was described as "He" or "Him." Paternalism was firmly entrenched. This edition of *Are You Running with Me, Jesus?* represents a sincere belief in the significance of inclusive language and an honest effort to utilize it.

I have written a number of new prayers that have found their way into this edition. Scattered intermittently throughout the book, they concern a wide range of subjects, including AIDS, the planet Earth, gridlock traffic in the city, the human voyage into space, a ceremony of loving union, the ongoing struggle for racial justice, and the plight of the new immigrants in our midst. And there are a few new chapters: Meditations at a Zen Buddhist Retreat in the Country; Meditations at Home, at Work, on Identity, on Curious Occasions, about Life and Death in a Retirement Home; Nonverbal Prayers; and Jesus Prayers.

In the pages of this book you will find meditations and reflections, fragments of experience and memory that express a yearning for wholeness, and many different forms of what we call prayer. The book is very specific about names, objects, places—and people. Whenever and wherever I have been able to discern universal meaning, it has been within the particular.

If you are willing to share the intimacy of a spiritual journey with me and let me be your guide in occasional labyrinths and over some hills, I offer you my hand.

MALCOLM BOYD

Prayers for the Free Self

It's morning, Jesus. It's morning, and here's that light and sound all over again

I've got to move fast . . . get into the bathroom, wash up, grab a bite to eat, and run some more.

I just don't feel like it. What I really want to do is get back into bed, pull up the covers, and sleep. All I seem to want today is the big sleep, and here I've got to run all over again.

Where am I running? You know these things I can't understand. It's not that I need to have you tell me. What counts most is just that somebody knows, and it's you. That helps a lot.

So I'll follow along, OK? But lead, please. Now I've got to run. Are you running with me, Jesus?

~ *I'm crying and shouting inside tonight, Jesus, and I'm feeling completely alone*

All the roots I thought I had are gone. Everything in my life is in an upheaval. I am amazed that I can maintain any composure when I'm feeling like this.

The moment is all that matters; the present moment is of supreme importance. I know this. Yet in the present I feel dead. I want to anchor myself in the past and shed tears of self-pity. When I look ahead tonight I can see only futility, pain, and death. I am only a rotting body, a vessel of disease, potentially a handful of ashes after I am burned.

But you call me tonight to love and responsibility. You have a job for me to do. You make me look at other persons whose needs make my self-pity a mockery and a disgrace.

Jesus, I hear you. I know you. I feel your presence strongly in this awful moment, and I thank you. Help me onto my feet. Help me to get up.

You said there is perfect freedom in your service, Jesus

Well, I don't feel perfectly free. I don't feel free at all. I'm a captive to myself.

I do what I want. I have it all my own way. There is no freedom at all for me in this, Jesus. Today I feel like a slave bound in chains and branded by a hot iron because I'm a captive to my own will and don't give an honest damn about you or your will.

You're over there where I'm keeping you, outside my real life. How can I go on being such a lousy hypocrite? Come over here, where I don't want you to come. Let me quit playing this blasphemous game of religion with you. Help me to let you be yourself in my life—so that I can be myself.

I know it sounds corny, Jesus, but I'm lonely

I wasn't going to get lonely any more, and so I kept very busy, telling myself I was serving you. But it's getting dark again, and I'm alone; honestly, Christ, I'm lonely as hell.

Why do I feel so sorry for myself? There's no reason why I should be. You're with me, and I know it. I'll be with other people in a little while. I know some of them love me very much in their own way, and I love some of them very much in mine.

But I still feel so damned lonely right now, in this minute that I'm living. I feel confused about how to get through the immediate next few steps to the other ones afterward. It's silly, but I feel this way because I'm threatened by me, and I wish I could get through to you, clearly and with a kind of purity and integrity.

And yet, while I say this to you, I've been unkind to certain people whom you also love, and I've added to misunderstanding and confusion, and I haven't been able to make it at all nicely or properly.

Take hold of me, and connect me with these other lives, Jesus. Give me patience and love so that I can listen when I plug into these other lives. Help me to listen and listen and listen . . . and love by being quiet and serving, and being there.

I'm scared, Jesus. You've asked me to do something I don't think I can do

I'm sure I wouldn't want to do it except that you asked me.

But I don't feel strong enough, and you know that I lack the courage I'd need. Why did you ask me to do this? It seems to me that Paul could do this much, much more easily. Remember, I told you I'm afraid to stand up and be criticized, Jesus. I feel naked in front of everybody, and I can't hide any part of myself.

Why can't I be quiet and have peace and be left alone? I don't see what good it will do for me to be dragged out in front of everybody and do this for you. Don't misunderstand me. I'm not saying I won't do it. I'm just saying I don't *want* to do it. I mean, how in hell *can* I do it?

You know me better than anybody does, but then you go and ask me to do something crazy like this. I can't figure you out. I wish you'd just leave me alone today, but if this is what you think is best, I'll try. I'll try. But I don't want to. Pray for me, Jesus.

The drinks are tranquilizing me, relaxing me and helping me to take it

But even while I'm being tranquilized, I don't want to be.

I remember the cutting edge you lived on. You didn't get tranquilized. You went right on taking it, and then you gave back love. I seem to have run out of love, and I'm certainly taking it very badly right now.

Don't leave me alone, Christ, because I've left you. I just want the easy way out, any way out at all, but you know I really don't. I hurt inside and wish I could tear myself away.

This isn't me here, Jesus. This really isn't me. You know it, but nobody else does. I'm putting on a good act, but you know what a lousy act it really is.

Get me back on my own cutting edge. Help me to put away the tranquilizers and just be myself with you and the others you place with me.

I feel great, and I just want to thank you, Jesus

This is a good day for me. Yesterday I was down, but today I'm up again. These people I'm with are loving and supportive. The sun has really come out for me. I see everything in bright reds and yellows.

I hated the dark reds and the crying blues yesterday. I was mean, Christ, and vicious, and I can hardly understand how anybody put up with me. But they didn't beat me down. They let me know what it is to be human because *they* stayed human. Now I'm human again. I feel good, and I want to get out with the people and swing with them.

There's somebody I was mean to yesterday. I want to knock myself out to be nice to him today. Honestly, Jesus, thank you.

I'm gripped and obsessed by hatred of someone, Jesus

Is it because we're alike? Does that mean I hate a part of myself? The situation is embarrassing because, although I don't like to be with this person, we must work together.

I'm baffled by myself. It seems unlike me to be so irrational, arrogant, unloving, out of control. What's the matter with me?

Should I meet this person and confess my feelings? I realize that a strong hatred is filled with passion. Do I feel love for this person in ways I simply can't understand?

A great gulf is growing wider between us. I'm trapped by my pride. Help me, Jesus. Acid rain is falling.

It was a seven-point quake at 10:47 A.M.

An unexpected phone call tersely canceled my future plans. I sat stunned, Jesus. Everything promising had just been taken for granted for a long time. I had clearly been on a roll, and the future looked bright. Now my plans were in shambles.

My strong ego was suddenly tamed. Self-confidence went out the window. I began to reach out to other people for support.

Life beckoned to me as a member of the human race, neither a star nor a solitary player. I'm grateful for the spiritual oxygen.

Thanks for taking hold of me when I needed it most, Jesus.

I feel that I'm facing a dark room, Jesus

Anyone in that space can see me clearly. I stand here, wholly vulnerable.

Is anyone really out there in the dark, Jesus? I hear no sound, see no sign. But I feel uneasy and sense closeness to someone silent, watching, and very near.

Why do I wait for someone to walk out of the darkness into my life, Jesus? Why don't I have the courage to walk into the darkness?

If there's someone in there who fears me, maybe I'm the forbidding one, Jesus. If so, please help me to share and communicate.

Give me the courage not to fear the darkness.

Death is somewhere up ahead, Jesus

Casting glances at me out of the corner of an eye, it waits for me.

But I'm not ready to leave the world's stage. Not yet. Let me play my roles in repertory, speak my lines, sing and dance. I want to read tomorrow morning's newspaper, answer a letter, make a fresh salad, meet a new friend, see a new film, and start a hot fire in the grate.

Let me live a while, I pray. Then, when death places its hand in mine, please stay with me, Jesus.

The Mozart Sonata in B-flat Major

for violin and piano is on the stereo. Otherwise, the room is silent.

I am in a moment of solitude. The sun and clouds through high windows make stark, fluid reflections on a white wall. An immense tree outside the window seems my nearest companion. It is older than I am and will outlive me.

What am I to do with this solitude, Jesus? I can let it project me outside or else sink deep inside myself. The journey into self, if I choose that way, seems like some strange desert: remote, arid, very hard, quite perplexing. I would rather take the way out of myself.

But I need to explore my inner world and do work there to liberate myself from the past.

Stay with me, Christ, on my inner journey.

I used to think I had forever to live

Life seemed to stretch out like an endless highway. There would be time for everything.

But when I found out today that Matt has AIDS, Jesus, I realized all of a sudden there's a real limit to life.

Not only Matt's. Mine too. Everybody's. Matt is a friend whom I love. I also love the world. It seems to me that in a real sense the world presently has AIDS. We need to heal it, all the people in it, and ourselves.

Maybe the best way, Jesus, is to love people—each other. Do you agree? Appreciate life and give thanks for it. Live each moment to the fullest. Be kind and generous. Offer warmth and nurturing in place of coldness and rejection. Identify evil within our hearts and seek help to change it into goodness.

Wouldn't it be healing, Jesus, to breathe in honesty and breathe out joy? Help me to breathe that way, Jesus.

~ I want to say thanks, Jesus

Anxiety had overtaken me. I'm surprised how faithless I was. Stress had set me up for a killing. I didn't ask you for help, but tried to handle the crisis by myself, and lost.

Everything blew up. When the smoke cleared I saw you standing there. I also saw how I had loused up my life by trying to play the major domo.

I can't make it without you, Jesus. Thanks for starting over with me again.

Prayers in the City

They're in a golden world, Jesus

They're having a party in a hotel suite which is elegant and located in the best hotel in the heart of the city. There's music, jewelry, glamor, gin, V.I.P. status, and POWER.

But nobody's having any fun. They're too busy sparring with one another in the POWER game which, tonight, is also the sex-and-booze tournament.

Everybody looks slick and, underneath tans and wigs, somewhat lonely. They're only observing the stiff protocol of small talk and ground rules. This informal gathering is as rigid as the court of Louis XIV, only the accents here are of Detroit, Houston, and Los Angeles.

The masks are on parade tonight, Jesus. The masks are smiling and laughing to cover up status anxieties and bleeding ulcers.

Tell us about freedom, Jesus.

It's a jazz spot, Jesus

He's a musician who works here. Jazz for him is art and life. This is the way he expresses himself, tells it as it is, hangs on, and climbs.

But the night-club world is a tough one if you want to be free and be yourself. It's interested in top stars and pop performers. Steady work and the buck go together, and both are somewhat elusive. At least, that's his experience.

It's late in here tonight, Jesus. The customers are listening over their drinks; they're getting scared because soon they'll have to go into the dark night outside. There won't be any music or Scotch or lights out there on the early-morning streets. If there was someplace to go, they'd leave, but this is the last place open.

The musician is wondering if they're hearing him at all through their listening. He has something to say, and he's saying it. It's about death and life, sex and hunger, knowing yourself and being known, the dream, the vision. He's looking at the people, right into their dead and alive eyes, and he wants them to hear him.

Does he know you hear him, Jesus?

Look up at that window where the old guy is sitting

See, he's half-hidden by the curtain that's moving a little in the breeze. That tenement—it's a poor place to have to live, isn't it, Jesus?

He is seated alone by a kitchen table and looking blankly out the window. He lives with his sister, who is away working all day. There is nothing for him to do. He doesn't have any money; all he has is time.

Who is he in my life, Jesus? What has he got to do with me? He's your brother, and you love him. What does this say to me, Christ? I don't know what sense I am supposed to make out of this. I mean, how can I possibly be responsible in any honest, meaningful way for that guy?

He just moved a short bit away from the window. Maybe he moved because he felt my eyes on him from the sidewalk down here. I didn't mean to embarrass him; I just wanted to let him know somebody understands he's alive and he's your brother, so he's not alone or lost. Does he know it, Jesus?

⌒ *This is a gay bar, Jesus*

It looks like any other bar on the outside, only it isn't. Men stand three and four deep at this bar—some just feeling a sense of belonging here, others making contacts for new partners.

This isn't very much like a church, Christ, but many members of the church are also here in this bar. Quite a few of the men here belong to the church as well as to this bar. If they knew how, a number of them would ask you to be with them in both places. Some of them wouldn't, but won't you be with them, too, Jesus?

I feel all alone in a traffic jam, Jesus

But I am not alone, of course. Several thousand other people are here, too. Yet I feel utterly solitary within the confines of my car.

Four lanes of the highway as far as my eyes can see are packed with cars unable to move. The standstill holds for miles ahead and behind. There is nothing I can do to change the situation.

At first I felt rage about my predicament. "Why is this happening again?" Then frustration. "I must get out of the city and move immediately to the country or a small town."

But now I begin to feel relaxed, almost euphoric. "It's rather nice not to be hurrying anywhere." I'm curiously reminded of when I had the measles as a kid, and got to stay at home in bed instead of going to school. There was snow and ice outside, but inside my room it was warm and cozy.

Here on the crowded highway, trapped in what had seemed an antihuman situation, suddenly I feel human, Jesus. Humanity surrounds me, huddled in cars as I am. I know myself as a part of an immense adventure that is shared.

The kids are smiling, Jesus, on the tenement stoop

The little girl is the oldest, and she's apparently in charge of the younger two, her brothers.

But suddenly she's crying and her two brothers are trying to comfort her. Now everything seems to be peaceful, and she's smiling again.

But what's ahead for them, Christ? Home is this broken-down dump on a heartless, tough street. What kind of school will they go to? Will it be hopelessly overcrowded? Will it be a place that breeds despair? Will it change these kids' happy smiles into angry, sullen masks they'll have to wear for the rest of their lives?

I look at their faces and realize how they are our victims, especially when we like to say they are beautiful children, but we don't change conditions that will make their faces hard and their hearts cynical.

Have these kids got a chance, Jesus? Will they know anything about dignity or love or health? Jesus, looking at these kids, I'm afraid for them and for all of us.

The old house is nearly all torn down, Jesus

What became of the people who used to live here? Where are they now, and what has happened to the roots they had here?

The demolition men are doing a good job. A week ago they started cold, and now the house is just about down. I saw them taking it down floor by floor, room by room. They tied a rope onto the wooden frames of rooms and pulled them, bringing them tumbling down onto the ground. Suddenly the derelict old house is nearly gone. In a day or so there will be only a patch of ground on a city block where people made love, men and women fought and relaxed and worked, babies were born, and death visited from time to time. It will be strange for people who used to live here when they come back home and there isn't any home.

Help us to learn how to live with mobility and rapid change and the absence of old securities, remembering that you didn't have any place to lay your head when you lived among us.

In this ugly red building, old people are waiting for death

They're inside, Jesus, two or three in a room, and three times a day other people bring them food to eat. Otherwise, they generally don't have anything to do except watch television.

Is this death for them now, Jesus? Do they know they will have life afterward, when they die? Their families must hate to come and see them in this ugly old house—is that why they hardly ever do?

But these old people in this old house—are they happy at all? Do they know you're in here with them and also that you have overcome the power and loneliness of death? Do they? I hope the doctors who come here to see them have a lot of patience and kindness, and that the nurses do too. Help everybody in that house to have a lot of patience and kindness, Jesus.

I know pity is useless, Jesus, but I can't help feeling sorry for her

She still has more writing talent than a dozen other people, but her life is going down the drain. She never learned how to live with her talent or use it. She starts drinking, and, when she gets tired of that, she takes heroin. She ran through most of the men in her life a long time ago.

But she always gives everybody that bright, energetic smile as if nothing was the matter, and she doesn't eat her heart out until she is alone. Her smile isn't jaded—she has a quality of innocence which is very real.

She gives with the assured patter she learned when she was enrolled in the best schools. She still wears clothes like the debutante she was fifteen years ago, although she has become very heavy and her coat is a rag. She lives in a run-down house in a slum. Her family is ashamed of her now and doesn't want anything to do with her.

Be good to her, please. She is so insecure and lost and needs your love badly. Of all your mixed-up loved ones, she is one of the saddest, even though she always wears this big smile. Jesus, underneath her tired, worn-out mask, let her know she is loved.

~ *He'll never work again, Jesus*

He's sitting there on the park bench and is just beginning to quit fighting the fact. He's only around forty, and he's had it because he doesn't have a skill, and automation has come.

But he's not making any sense out of all this. His wife goes off to work in the mornings as a domestic; and the two kids are in school; the other one is in the service.

Instead of being the leader of his family he's nothing, Jesus, nothing at all. He can sit at home and look at television, but that gets boring; anyway, he's a man and wants to be a man. When his wife brings home the money she earns he's belligerent, and takes some of it to buy booze so he can forget for a little while.

The kids despise him. When he pulls rank with them, he feels less like a man or a human being than at any other time. He feels left out of things, forgotten, a human hulk in a bright, flashing world of machines and successful men. The sheen of success isn't on him. He looks seedy and tired and washed out.

What is he to do, Jesus? What is his family to do? What am I to do, standing here, looking on?

Everybody says he's going places

See him over there, driving the new blue car? He's in a hurry to get home so he can get ready to go out again.

He's always in a hurry, Jesus. He knows what he wants and how to get it. His future in business is carefully mapped out. He's a young executive, and lives in the right neighborhood, belongs to the right clubs, and attends the right church.

But he feels awfully threatened, Jesus, by a lot of things and people. He doesn't see why his world can't remain secure, old-fashioned, traditional, and white. If some foreigners in Africa or Asia or Latin America are causing trouble, he doesn't see why America doesn't really stand up to its enemies, because then there would be peace and security.

Reading the newspaper disturbs him. If only something could be done by the government about some of the problems—the spread of Communism, violence in our cities, black and Latino people claiming equality with whites—then he could see more point to his working so hard for security.

He's looking out of his car window. Does he see persons, or just things? Does he see you standing on the street, Jesus?

Meditations at a Zen Buddhist Retreat in the Country

A long rattlesnake slides by me. Less than three feet away, it moves quickly, resolutely, easily

I am seated beneath a tree in the shade. Below, a mountain stream plunges noisily into a natural pool. I was meditating when the snake suddenly appeared.

What am I to do? Snakes, I've always been told, are dangerous things. Yet here it seems to fit into a context. I've hiked for more than a steady half-hour up into the hills to this place. But doesn't the snake have the same rights of possession that I do?

In a certain sense, I am aware, neither of us has rights. The earth is not ours to own. Yet in another very practical sense, the earth is given to each of us in a certain moment to use and enjoy. We have the right to be ourselves as God made us.

The snake slides ahead, hopefully enjoying its day, occupying its space in our common life, doing what is natural for a rattlesnake to do on a summer day. I sit here, watch it move, return to my meditation. I realize with a start: *it* has become my meditation.

To reach the rapids far up the stream, one must embark on a small journey

First, there is the stream to cross on a fragile wooden board. Tippety-top, tippety-top: Why does the board wobble? Will I be able to make it?

Yes. But soon the stream must be criss-crossed, this time by jumping or stepping from rock to rock. It is a precarious business. These rocks are not easy to follow. Some are large or small, wobbly or slick, a few barely below water level.

Clip-clop, clip-clop, I walk beside the stream for a while. Now it's time again to cross, trying to find my way on uneasily perched rocks that can give way unexpectedly. Ahead there is yet a third stream crossing. I slip and bloody my knee. Why did this happen to me? Is it my place in life always to be the one who falls on unsure rocks? I am obsessed for a moment by self-pity.

However, survival comes first. There is a rock slide area to be traversed. This is a real workout and I am breathing hard. After this comes a slippery ledge to climb. If I miss my footing . . . but I cannot.

Finally, I've come to the rapids. It seems to me life is a strange, impermanent journey leading through manifold changes to stages.

I fall asleep alongside a stream

The sound is as loud as a train, but lulls me. I curl up, use a towel for a pillow, and am gone into an inner journey. Leaves on a tree overhead filter hot sunlight.

After a while—I've no idea of time, have left behind my watch—I awaken. I am startled, but also comforted, to hear the rush of water only a few feet away from my feet. I watch the water cascade over rocks, plunge into a swirling pool, then make a slide that resembles a waterfall.

This makes so much more sense than bumper-to-bumper traffic on a highway, high-density population, polluted air, and an urban center's noise level. At this precise moment I do not miss the theater, cinema, a fine restaurant, a distinguished newspaper, or the company of stimulating people.

I curl up again, my towel making an exquisite pillow, and am shortly asleep. This sleep heals psychic wounds, illumines encrusted corridors of my mind, softens harsh anxieties and fears, brings me home to the life within.

Riding the crest of a fast-flowing stream, I feel like a tiny leaf

Being physical like this is such a change for me, an inbred city person. Here, I climb over huge rocks, lose my way, sweat and thirst, and lose my breath.

I allow the racing stream to take me on a roller-coaster slide. It swerves left to right, right to left, and deposits me, plop, in a natural pool. To my genuine surprise, I find that I am still here—all right, healthy, among the living. The water is icy cold. Tiny fishes swim around me, coming close to smell. Baptized in the water, I become a convert.

It occurs to me something remarkable has taken place: I have given up control.

I feel bitterness and rage

It is my first night here in the country, and I cannot let go of my emotions. I want revenge. I want someone whom I feel has wronged me to suffer for it.

I toss and turn in the bed. I'm aware of the beauty and holiness surrounding me, yet refuse to yield to their nurturing and purity. So, I relive a memory. Insult is added to hurt; communication has broken down between people; a partly real, partly imagined, hurt festers.

Moving back into the memory, someone whom I love is maligned by someone else who resorts to self-destruction and madness. It had all been meant to be a lovely evening, an occasion of warm joy. I remember bitterly its savage twisting into a murderous charade. Now I am overwhelmed by anger and rage.

Seductively, gradually, the beauty and holiness that surround me in this country place assert their power over me. I embrace them sensuously, to move inside a peaceful, deep sleep.

The first night here, I found people so difficult

I wanted the retreat to be simply my own. *My* peace is what seemed significant; *my* satisfaction and quiet time, *my* spiritual gratification, *my* way.

Now I've begun to look around at the others with a new view. They're interesting. They show their wounds. They're human.

Clearly, all of us are looking for something here. Perhaps we can find it together. Self-interest becomes interest in one another. Some of us came here to get away, others to draw close; we need to merge our intentions.

Last night, the leader of the Zen community spoke about Buddhist precepts, about dharma. Those of us seated in the room were drawn into a sense of mutuality. I was made to realize I want to be a better person, less thorny and complex, more open and willing to engage others and the unexpected.

⤼ *This is the blue jays' empire*

One hears the bird chatter until night falls when the crickets take over. The blue jays are loud and combative. Other birds seem to have been vanquished or banished. Could a new army of eagles start a bird war?

But why would anyone wish a war of any kind here? Roses bloom. Vegetables grow. Fresh breads are baked. There is no electricity; kerosene lamps make a gentle light. One goes to sleep early. Before evening light fades, a hillside fills my view through a cabin window, with the sole exception of a tiny patch of sky in the right corner.

In the morning I hear blue jays again. Only now they seem harbingers of a peaceable reign. I am convinced one of them is speaking directly to me. What shall I respond?

These words are found at the entrance of the Zen bathhouse

With all beings
I wash body and mind
Free from dust
Pure and shining
Within and without

I draw a tub full of hot water and bathe leisurely, shave, and wash my hair. Afterwards I move to a pool of hot sulphur water, relax, and meditate. Soon I visit the steam room. Finally I immerse myself in the icy cold water of the stream a few steps away.

So many thoughts of anxiety, stress and fears had polluted my mind and consciousness. While cleansing my body, I concentrate on the simple sound of running water. I let the water flow through my thoughts and feelings to cleanse me within.

I awaken

Sleeping on my side, my head turned on a pillow, I hear my heartbeat. It is clear, direct. However, I find it troubling and obtrusive, for it reminds me in the inky darkness of my mortality.

Surrounded by earth's stillness and sounds, I freely accept the reality that I came from the earth and will return to it. Still, I don't find warmth or friendliness in the specter of mortality. It is an unwelcome ghost.

I move my head to avoid hearing my heartbeat. Instead I listen to the sound of running water. Yet I remember what a Zen instructor said about treating unwanted sound in an inclusive manner, letting it enter. He recommended not trying to repress it, but actually concentrating on it.

I turn my head on the pillow and listen to my heartbeat.

Meditations at Home

I cut up onions, garlic, and mushrooms, and place them in a large pan on the stove

My spaghetti sauce is underway. It's restful to cook when I don't feel the pressure of a deadline. I just putter, pouring oregano and basil as if I were an alchemist, stir the ingredients, add meat, fresh tomatoes, and tomato sauce. Grated cheese stands ready.

The simmering mix seems to make a nurturing and comfortable sound in the quiet kitchen. The stove is transformed into a holy altar of life. What I am cooking is not a work of art that will claim a lasting place or excite human admiration for long. One of life's small pleasures, it will be gobbled up gratefully and forgotten.

Yet this is a special task for me. It's unselfish, compared to many things I do; truly an offering to a few friends. It's meticulous work; a right or wrong decision can be crucial. I reach for the tarragon.

I find it a sacred time of kitchen meditation to stir, smell, add, taste, grate, ponder, and let simmer.

I am doing the wash

The washer industriously whirrs away while the dryer amiably tumbles a load. I pour detergent in the bottom to get the wash started, and also clean the screen in the dryer. I place sheets in the bottom of the washer, with towels on top.

Then I sit down to read, but can't concentrate because I know it will be necessary shortly to unload the dryer, transfer the finished wet laundry in the washer to the dryer, and place a new batch in the washer. I try to think of a short-range project to do in this limited amount of time, and fail.

Doing the wash isn't exactly a momentous feat. It won't get written up in the newspaper or make the six o'clock news, or even elicit particular comment. This seems grossly unfair. Doing the wash is far more essential than lots of things going on today at City Hall, cleaner than ward politics, better for the world than making MX missiles.

Housecleaning is a ritual

Open windows! Let in fresh air! Bustle and clean carpets and cushions, mop floors, wash windows, dust, cleanse, sweep!

Housecleaning is good for the soul. It gives one something practical to do. The body and soul are working together. One can see results before one's eyes.

But be sure to get into every cranny and corner with a broom, a brush, a rag. Wipe glass covering pictures hanging on walls. Shake dust. Cleanse counters. Wash dishes. Take down draperies and curtains. Water tile floors, make them shine.

Doing this, I know instinctively that I must also engage myself soon in a seasonal housecleaning of the soul. Yes. This, without undue delay.

I water the garden

It is a good feeling of companionship with the earth to help it sustain life.

I soak the dry grass, make a special effort to revitalize a bougainvillea plant that is sick, and spray expectant pansies lightly so that I will not bruise them.

The plant over in the corner that is hard to reach was ailing, but seems to be doing well now. A huge, healthy bush needs to be pruned soon. Small plants in a big pot await my attention.

It's lovely here. Wind chimes sing out in a cool breeze. I marvel at the patience of the plants and flowers. The gentle way they respond to love is touching. Can I learn?

I see a cockroach

I'd rather see a Martian standing in my home today. Does this mean there's a horde of roaches waiting in the winds like Atilla the Hun and his followers? Or is this a sole cockroach—a courageous innovator, a wiry loner?

Am I compelled to commit murder this afternoon, or may I be magnanimous?

Who, I wonder, decides what creatures are accepted as a part of life, and what creatures aren't? Sometimes humans find themselves in the same position. I look at the cockroach; it looks at me. Clearly, it's a very specific form of creation, as I am. It appears to be intricate, complex and mysterious.

At least for today, I make a decision to place cockroach rights ahead of the status quo. Can't God's creatures appreciate one another?

Friends come to dinner

What a delight. Ted and Bruce, Carrie and Ruth, Elaine and Bill. We prepare a buffet and everyone sits around the fireplace to eat, juggling plates and glasses of wine.

I wonder if friends know how much they contribute to a home by coming into it. They add other presences, joining familiar pictures, books, dishes, chairs, and plants to make a scene. If all the world's a stage, a scene has its own value. A scene like this, not caught on film, will linger in the consciousness.

Ted and Ruth chat about politics, Carrie and Elaine discuss a new film, Bill and Bruce talk about themselves and their lives.

Such a civilized ritual. Such a warm celebration of friendship. Such a holy gift to be together here.

The home is ours,

yours and mine. We share it. We share so many other things because of it.

Yet the home is not simply ours. It is also *yours,* also *mine.* You are, and need to be, completely at home here. So do I. This introduces compromise. I do not encroach on your rights to be fulfilled and happy in your home; neither do you in mine.

The answer is found in mutuality, the sharing of the home as *ours.* This calls for common tasks, responsibilities, things to do from mopping floors to washing clothes, cooking to vacuuming, putting out garbage to watering the garden.

It also means comforting each other; creating pleasure and beauty, warmth and coolness in season, lively scenes of entertainment and quiet ones of reflection.

I cannot think of the home as mine. I love sharing it with you, and having you share it with me—and the selfish/unselfish, magnanimous sharing of ourselves.

I sit quietly by the fireplace, drink a cup of tea, read a book

I love the home. I know my way around it by heart; where to place my foot on what step in the dark, how to locate a step or a spoon without thinking.

A home should never become an illusion of a security it cannot offer. I know that, and am grateful for the knowledge. Still, this home is a sanctuary of sorts, a temple of shared experience, feelings, and love.

I drift off for a moment, but catch myself and awaken sharply. I take a sip of tea, my energy snaps back, and I return to my reading. A log burning in the fireplace snaps. The silence inside the house is friendly, as are the ghosts.

I gather the friendliness around me like a blanket. It is important to sustain a hearth of love in a world of too much hate.

The time has come to move that picture on the wall

It's important, I decide, to do new things, take risks. Everything has been too settled around here for a long time. But where shall I place it?

Over there near the bookcase. Only that means I'll have to move the bookcase, and the couch, and that table, and the plants. It's worth it. The room will look much better, have a fresh ambience.

I move the bookcase, and the couch, and that table, and the plants. I place the picture in its new location. I like it.

However, I've no idea what to put on the wall in the spot where the picture used to hang. The empty space mocks me, ridicules my impulsive ingenuity.

It's easier to leave everything where it already belongs, not to change or move a picture, isn't it? But I *will* move a picture.

Jesus, help me to take risks.

I am quite ill, have a fever

It paralyzes my senses. I don't have the will or strength to get out of bed. I can scarcely turn my body over.

The fever is like an electric current moving behind my eyes, in my limbs. Just lying here in bed, scarcely breathing, without making any physical exertion at all, is all I can do. I have a capacity for sleep like a blotter for ink.

I took health for granted, didn't I? Jesus, please be my healer.

I ponder the meaning of my life

I know there is a face, a smile, and a frown. There is passion, a residue of rage, and an icy capacity to withdraw. There is the familiar body, the uncharted mind, and the chameleon performing as a clown.

I know there is a tenderness, a warmth, and a biting revenge that reacts to real or imaginary hurt. There is the man-woman, child, and the indelible image of God that calls to me in what I know as a conscience. There is a hunger that is insatiable, a thirst that burns and gnaws, and a hard selfishness that can be cruel.

I know there is a vaulting amibition, a complex drive that will not let me rest, and a laziness made for a summer's day. There is an idealism that can startle my self-interest, a sense of duty that can suffocate ticklish inclinations toward abandon, and a ruthless sense of self-sovereignty that can arrogantly try to bluff even Almighty God.

I know there is a cultivated self-sufficiency, a suicidal loneliness, and a dreaded anxiety. There is a personal history with tears and laughter, a public life, and a being so vulnerable that it can be smashed into pieces like a glass.

What is there in me of holiness, Jesus? What is there within me possessing hidden life that cannot be broken or burned or obliterated? What is there of me that is love?

You became human, Jesus. As a man you experienced loneliness, anger, joy, depression and hope.

Thank you for being human like me, Jesus.

Meditations at Work

Why won't noon get here?

Concentration seems to be my big problem today. I'm not doing it. Instead I'm allowing all kinds of thoughts and problems, big ones and small, to filter through. I need to make a list of priorities, and follow it from top to bottom.

If I could just get out of here for a few minutes, take a walk, clear my head. I need to focus.

Suddenly, I realize I can sit right here and do that. I take a moment to center myself. The many competing, shouting voices inside me start to quiet down. I breathe consciously, knowingly, fill my lungs with air, release it slowly.

Equilibrium is restored. I can smile honestly at a certain awareness: As important as all this is, it isn't *that* important. What a difference it makes to know that.

My phone keeps ringing

It's one of those mornings in the office when one impossible problem after another seems to come up. People I haven't heard from in a year are back in touch, each with a question or a crisis.

A stranger demands to see me immediately about a matter that doesn't fit my talent, skills, or role at work. A rumor surfaces (I hear it on my way to the men's room) that the head of the office may leave to take another job. Another rumor (it comes to my ears at lunch) says the company is in a financial hubbub.

"Hello. Yes, I am. *Good* to hear from you, but . . ." Two calls are backed up on the line, waiting for me. This is when stress beckons like an old childhood friend, panic buttons start to get pushed. "I think this is going to take a bit more time than we can manage on the phone. Do you suppose we can arrange a meeting to talk?"

A long-distance call I've been awaiting since last Monday is on the line. But I've got to terminate *this* call, and someone is talking, talking, talking . . .

Calm me down, Jesus. Please quiet me and give me your wisdom and strength.

Clark started to shout at me

He had come into my office, closed the door, and angrily confronted me. I was absolutely surprised. His face got red and he talked so rapidly he didn't stop to take a breath.

Clark has long been my closest work friend. On various occasions he has drifted into my office to share the most intimate life details, yearnings, plans, opinions.

But today he seemed vicious in things he said. We had never fought before and he had never indicated any hostility toward me. Abruptly, he fell silent and sat down. In a moment he held his head in his hands, and cried.

His marriage, he explained, seemed to be on the rocks. Although he's been under extraordinary stress for several weeks, he felt unable to share his feelings about it before this morning.

Simple communication between people is such a mystery to me, Jesus. When Clark stood there, enraged and shouting at me, it had nothing to do with me at all. Help me to remember this, Jesus. Help me to remember this.

My work makes me ask: What is effectiveness, Jesus?

Some people place it ahead of honesty. But without honesty, wouldn't something just appear on the surface to be effective? It would really be a failure.

Success and failure seem to be badly misunderstood, don't they? They are judged by outward appearances instead of inner realities. I have felt deep failure at moments when people said I was a success. I have felt fulfilled and successful as a human being when I was most severely judged to be a failure.

You have taught us, Jesus, that a person can gain the whole world and lose one's soul. This seems to be true for whole nations and societies, and business firms, too. Do we hear what you are saying?

He's gossiping again about other people who work here

I can always tell when Brian gets that glint in his eyes, walks into my office, and shuts the door. Then he starts to dish about someone in particular or nearly everybody in general. I can imagine what he says about me behind my back.

It depresses me and drains my energy to hear him spew out his apparent dislike of other people here. Afterwards, when my eyes meet *theirs,* I feel guilty that I even heard all the lies and fantasies about them.

I've told Brian several times not to share his gossip with me, but it does no good; he seems not to hear. Gossip is to him what booze is to an alcoholic.

He opens all the available sewers to let his germs spread. The danger is that he spreads his distorted, hateful, envious views of others. So, Brian's views take on a life of their own. He gives them life.

When he ridicules and cuts people to ribbons, I try to combat him by seeing the people in their fantastic human beauty and wholeness.

Should I get out of here before they fire me?

I am having an anxiety attack today. For one thing, I am aware I'm growing older—am I also out of touch with new ideas, trends, ways of looking at things?

It seems to me I should be making more money. When I visited a supermarket yesterday and saw my bill at the checkout counter, I laughed bitterly at claims that inflation has been licked. On my salary, how can I afford to live as I want? I know I couldn't manage for any length of time without this job. Should I try to get another that pays more?

For a long time, it seems, I haven't actually been challenged in this job. I feel the need of a bracing new challenge. Am I growing stale? Is this more apparent to others than me? Do I *need* a move?

All of us here are locked in a routine that has become rote. We do the same things over and over—rather well, yes, but frankly, I'm bored today. What can I do? Where do I belong? I could jump out of my skin.

My perspective of self and others is blurred and distorted. I can't see the forest for the trees, Jesus. I need your help with my vision today.

I heard today about Larry's death, Jesus

My first reaction was sadness because such an honest man and good companion in our day-by-day life at the office was gone from the scene. I'll miss him. It seemed to me he always went out of his way to do the best he could about people and things.

He made an effort to find out the truth and didn't spare himself in the process. He took an unpopular stand when his beliefs called for it and never seemed to court an easy or sham popularity. He was a loyal friend but also an honest one in offering direct criticism, even when it hurt to give and receive it.

I know how lonely his wife will be now and how much she will miss him. Bless his death and resurrection in you, Jesus. Bless his wife's sorrow and stirring of new life.

I was startled to find out Norma is leaving

She has been on the job five years. So have I.

Her decision to resign and take another job is like a small death to me. She has become as much a part of my life as, it seems odd to say, some members of my family.

I have never seen Norma without buoyancy and the ability to laugh. Over the years we have created funny, crazy situations for each other—absurd Valentines, practical jokes, embellished office reports that became hilarious.

More important, she has been something of a sister to me. Norma has listened to me talk about my real fears and human problems. She's never been judgmental, offers helpful advice and the gift of time and energy.

Her going away creates a great void in my life. How can I tell her how much she means to me without sounding stupidly sentimental?

Jesus, help me fill this void of loneliness at work.

I'm working late

I decided to stay here, do an office housecleaning—work my way through the stack of papers on my desk.

It's a luxurious feeling to be able to do this slowly, knowing I have plenty of time. My office phone won't ring. Mail won't come. A colleague won't stand at my door, waiting to talk.

What an odd, not unwelcome, sensation to be alone here. It raises strange thoughts. For example, I realize the impersonal office isn't mine, although this is my second home eight hours a day. I look around at the pictures, books, and personal items I've brought in to create a sense of belonging. All these could be removed arbitrarily; they will one day.

This line of thought evokes a sense of my own mortality. I will be removed one day, too. However, in the moment at hand I am gratefully alive. I'll try to make the best of both gifts, life and work.

The stack of papers that cluttered my desk has nearly disappeared, some into files, other pieces into a trash basket. The top of my desk is nearly clean.

~ *This staff meeting is entirely too long*

If Lucille, who has the floor, could relax and laugh, and willingly give up some control, it would be easier for everybody. She has an apparent need to dominate and insist on her own way without compromise or give-and-take. It's troubling.

I look at Ernie and can see he's on one of his roller-coaster mood swings. When Ernie is up, dozens of new projects are dizzying in the air. When he's down, the brooding silence around him is an environment for a jungle war. This morning Ernie is down.

Bad. Because everything seems on edge in the office so far today. Egos are twisted out of shape unbearably. Roger, ordinarily laidback, seems a veritable Niagara Falls, a super-charged workaholic, an obtrusive stranger who can't keep his mouth shut. My God, I'm *tired.* Why did I get up?

Looking around the room, I wonder how the others see *me* this morning. Do I look as preposterous as they do to me? My face breaks into a smile. I'm aware how close I came to losing my sense of humor.

I realize this is the only work community I have. It's a good community, filled with real people, essential to my life. I offer thanks for it.

Meditations on Curious Occasions

~ *Mike, my dog, was dying on that rainy day*

I had often wondered about the relationship between Mike and the human world. How he had looked at life, houses, shops from a speeding car, lights in tall buildings at night, authority and freedom, the human schedule he had grown accustomed to, squirrels and cats—and me.

Mike, who was sixteen years old, somehow got to his feet and stood beside me. I reached out to touch the head and body of a close companion before he died.

Thank you for the mystery, the simplicity and wonder, of the relationship between Mike and me, Jesus.

I went with some children to the zoo yesterday

It was a nice morning; the wind was brisk, the sun shining. The children had old friends to call upon so I followed along. First we saw the rhinoceros. There were some rhinoceros babies, too, and all of us exchanged greetings with them. Next we went to see the hippopotamus family. Everybody looked at everybody else for a while, some of us outside cages, others inside. There seemed to be a sense of mutual liking and acceptance.

Then we visited the walrus. It was an incredible ham, zooming through the water on its back, turning hand flips, coming up for fish and applause, suddenly disappearing beneath dramatically turbulent waves. I could identify easily with the walrus, for I have often fantasized such behavior in my own bathtub.

I saw the man on the moon

His face looked very full to me when I was a kid. He wore a grin of sorts. I considered him benign, a little foolish, certainly harmless. Why he was up there, I had no idea. But I used to look at him and wonder.

Later I heard the face wasn't a face at all, only canals and rivers and mountains making a pattern. I was sorry to lose the human touch up in the sky with the stars at night, but frankly I didn't worry about it. Finally when astronauts went into space and landed on the moon, I saw them walking around.

What new surprises await me in space, Jesus? Help me to get ready for them, and understand.

I heard a man cry out in terrible pain or anguish

I awaken suddenly—and realize I am coming out of a dream.

The cry rang out from deep inside me. I am aware the man who cried out is a part of myself. He is trying to reach "me." He wishes to communicate, move from entombment inside myself, enter freely into my consciousness, come into "my" life.

He is a part of my inner life, which I have come to know in my dreams. I spend so much time and energy in my outer life, yet the inner one is also compelling, real, holds answers to questions about meaning.

I am grateful for the call to wholeness in my dreams, Jesus; the challenging reality of my inner journey through the pilgrimage of life. Thanks for bringing together the lost fragments of my life, Jesus, calling me to truth and you.

How machinelike can humans become?

It's a hot day. Driving down a hill, I see the backs of a dozen or more cars ahead. Their rear lights flash on—red! click!—then a few feet farther they turn off. Now on again—red! click!—off. On. Off. On. Off. On off. Fifty times going down the winding hill road.

My lights are doing the same thing, Jesus, as I place my foot on the brake and take it off. On. Off. Am I operating the machine or is it really operating me? Everybody else looks funny, I think, sitting inside the plain or brightly colored machines they are driving.

A lot of machines and people seem to look alike. The appearances of the people seem to fit the personalities of the cars they have selected. Do I look like my car? I may even behave like it. A question forms in my mind. Why do machines sometimes behave like the worst humans, and humans like the worst machines?

I'm with you in a television studio, Jesus

A star is out there in front right now, and the audience is responding with laughter. I'm a guest, nervously waiting to go on. People working with cameras, lights, and props, the director and her assistants, a publicity woman—they're all hard at work. Ad specialists are checking copies of the commercials, and sponsors are watching in distant offices and homes.

Do all these people know you're here too, Christ? Would they willingly and knowingly present you with this show, along with their motives for working on it?

Thanks for being with all of us here in the studio, Jesus.

I've got *to get into the left lane* now, *Jesus*

All the energy of my life is suddenly focused on this sole objective. For the past few seconds my left turn signal has been blinking, but no one has let me into the lane on this crowded highway. Now the intersection where I must turn is only a few feet away.

Cars speed past. A sense of panic seizes me. Perhaps I'm somehow out of place here and can't compete. Is this such a deadly business as it seems, or do we all know we're playing a child's game? If I can't get into the lane, I'll be quite late. It's madness. The highway doesn't belong to anyone driving on it. Why must I fight for the small space I need, Jesus?

The system has to work. I know that. If it falls apart here, it can't be depended on anywhere. I see inches to spare in front of the speeding car coming up on my left. I swerve over. The car slackens its pace. Now it pulls back, easily and deliberately. I have found a friend.

Sitting in the theater, I can scarcely wait for the lights to dim

Here I am in my anonymity. I feel shut off from every distraction. The screen is remote, *up there,* and I'm down here, able to relate or not relate to it as I choose.

The film has begun. It is telling a story, and concerns persons. Now I recognize myself. I'm up there, too, Jesus, involved in trying to make a decision. It's painful and I'm suffering.

I feel the closeness of other persons near me in the theater. I'm not suffering alone. We are so naked, Jesus, sitting here together and seeing ourselves (and each other) up there. Only the story isn't *up there* any more. It's *here.*

When the lights come up, and the movie has ended, will we remember anything of our closeness, or will we all be sitting quite alone? At first I wanted both escape and communion inside this theater. Now I know I can't escape, Jesus, and also how much I need communion.

Today she is seventy years old, Jesus

Everybody else is concerned about her birthday celebration while she is cooking breakfast and planning a visit to the grocery store.

It doesn't seem possible to her that she is seventy. Where did the years go? Her interests and thoughts are very young ones, moving backward swiftly over many years.

Where did the last week go so quickly? The last day—the last hour? Time is running through a sieve.

But, of course, she is not bound by it. She is free. Fear is merely a word. She sees her mother and father. Remember the picnic when she turned ten years old? She sees her college roommate and her Latin teacher and her husband and her baby and . . .

Somebody is telephoning to wish her a happy birthday.

She doesn't understand why nobody seems to realize how young she really is, Jesus.

✑ *David says he prays without being aware of it when he paints, Jesus*

He says this is the real link that keeps him creating and able to function as an artist.

Is this true? Can David's painting be praying? If so, is it possible Richard prays in his social work studies, and Ruth when she edits her magazine . . . Bob while he types letters, and Estelle when she cleans people's apartments?

Help me to pray that way, too. I want to pray in my doing and being, Jesus.

⌔ *Christmas Eve*

Outside the window the afternoon light is fading. I'll sit here in the quiet for a few moments before I light the Christmas tree, turn on a lamp.

Other Christmas Eves crowd into my mind. How can I understand Christmas Eve, Jesus, beneath the tinsel and music, wrapping of presents, and pictures everywhere of you as a baby in a manger?

These next few hours—will I simply feel emptiness and longing? Try to cover them up with laughter and bright lights? But I want to feel the deep meaning of this night.

Tell me, what was Christmas Eve like?

Prayers for the Free Society

My body and the planet Earth are closely connected, Jesus

Hiking on a mountain pass, I see the lacework intricacy of your creation in the trees, leaves, foliage, stones, flowers, dirt, mud, glimpses of the sky above, and the sounds of birds singing near me.

Walking early in the morning on a beach, I share it with a distant figure holding a fishing pole. The energy of the ocean leaps out at me in the mystery of its waves and the earthy, roaring sound coming from the deep within its being. Standing here, I am grateful for the harmony of life that is your creation. The beach is my church, and I give thanks for the existence of ultimate goodness in your Spirit.

I take watchful care of my body, as you know. I exercise, eat foods that are nutritious, deal creatively with stress whenever I can, and realize I am the steward of my body.

But what can I do to maintain the health of the planet Earth? I see clearly that human greed endangers it. Its oceans and rivers are polluted, its ozone layer depleted,forests and wildlife are threatened, resources laid waste by developers and exploiters. Its cities, including mine, are being strangled.

The planet Earth is where you lived and died, isn't it, Jesus? Your thirty-three years were spent on its soil. You ate its bread and fruit and fish, drank its water and wine. You knew and loved its people, strode along a quiet beach under its moon, watched its sun rise and fall, lingered in its wilderness, and climbed its hills.

Awaken us, Jesus, to preserve this planet that we have shared together. Stir up our love and courage to

save the oceans
save the forests
save the farms
save the towns and cities
save the rivers and lakes
save the mountains and hills
save the flowers and trees
save the animals and wildlife
save us

↼ *What was Hiroshima like, Jesus, when the bomb fell?*

What went through the minds of mothers, what happened to the lives of children, what stabbed at the hearts of men when they were caught up in a sea of flame?

What was Auschwitz like, Jesus, when the crematoriums belched the stinking smoke from the burned bodies of people? When families were separated, the weak perished, the strong faced inhuman tortures of the spirit and the body. What was the concentration camp like, Jesus?

Tell us, Christ, that we, the living, are capable of the same cruelty, the same horror, if we turn our back on you, our brother, and our other sisters and brothers. Save us from ourselves; spare us the evil of our hearts' good intentions, unbridled and mad. Turn us from our perversions of love, especially when these are perpetrated in your name. Speak to us about war, and about peace, and about the possibilities for both in our very human hearts.

We know you love the world that you created and redeemed

We who stand in the world offer ourselves and our society for your blessing and healing.

We confess that we have failed to love as you did. We have been socially unjust, and our society is imperfect, fragmented, and sometimes sick to death.

Teach us your ways in the world and in this life which we share together. Don't let us restrict you to a narrow ghetto labeled "religion," but lead us to worship you in the fullness of life.

Give us light to seek true morality, not in narrow legalisms but in sacrifice and open responsibility. Show us how to express our love for you in very specific, human service to other people.

Jesus, change our hearts from hearts of stone to hearts of flesh, and let us give thanks to you for all of life.

Ann has AIDS and is dying, Jesus

She worries a lot about what will happen to her kids when she dies. Ann has had a long struggle and fought courageously. What disturbs me most is that I feel her death isn't really necessary, Jesus. If there had been public awareness when AIDS began, money had been poured into research, politicians had quit playing it safe with prejudice and treated AIDS as the health crisis it is, thousands of deaths like Ann's might have been prevented. How can I forgive this deathly and public sin, Jesus?

Can thousands of more lives be saved now, Jesus, if we all wake up and exert full energy to defeat AIDS?

Please *wake* us up, Jesus.

Work for him means hell, Jesus

He's well paid. He never works up a sweat. His task is a relatively simple one—in fact, he doesn't see the connection between it and anyone else's task and any kind of a completed product. Between his work and the end result—a new car—there seems to be nothingness, a big void, an assembly line to oblivion.

Some joker at a union meeting one night said something corny about discovering the "Christian meaning" of work. He'd like to put that Christian talker on the assembly line for exactly three months, day by day, hour after hour. What would the guy have to say *then* about "Christian meaning"?

His work is monotony to the point that he sometimes thinks he'll fall asleep—that, or start running wild down the assembly line. His work on the line affects his whole life, Jesus. *All* of it seems to be a mean, devilish assembly line—getting up, driving to work, eight hours on the job, rest breaks and lunch, driving home, looking at television, eating and sleeping. A fiery hell would be an exciting prospect for him to look forward to.

Can he be brought to life, Jesus? What could life and his work really mean to him?

She doesn't feel like an animal, Jesus, even though she's being treated like one

She looks sixty but she isn't yet forty years old. She is a migrant farm worker. She's working in this field all day—and day here means sunrise to sunset. Afterward, she'll go back with her family to spend the night in a one-room tin shack most people wouldn't let their dog live in.

Nothing seems to be gained by her suffering and deprivation, Jesus. She never gets ahead financially. The small amount of money taken in is already owed for groceries. She needs a lot of medical care she'll never receive. Her husband is just as much a beast of burden as she. Their children seem already to be caught in the same vicious circle of exploitation.

There is still a vision of humanness inside her mind and soul, Jesus, although her body is broken and her face is wasted. Should she nourish any glimmer of hope, or would it be better for her to erase hope from her consciousness? What happens to a society that takes such a toll in human life and doesn't care?

Somebody forgot to push the right button, Jesus

So all hell broke loose. Airline schedules are loused up, somebody is shouting at somebody else who can't help the situation, a lot of money has been lost, and about two dozen people are caught up in a cybernetic tangle. We've missed our plane, which isn't our fault, and I was due in Chicago to participate in a meeting forty-five minutes ago.

Please cool everybody off, including me, since I'm one of the people involved, and I'm hot right now and shouting angrily at someone else who can't help the cybernetic crisis any more than I can.

And, Jesus, please keep us human and capable of weathering such minor—and major—disasters. Don't let us turn ourselves into machines, no matter how hard we seem to be trying.

I've searched for community in many places, Jesus

I was often looking in the wrong places, but I don't think my motive was altogether wrong. I was looking futilely and hopelessly there for belonging and acceptance.

Now, in this moment, which many people would label "loneliness," or "nothingness," I want to thank you, Jesus. In this moment—in this place and with these other persons—I have found community where and as it is. It seems to me it is your gift.

I am here with these others for only a few hours. I will be gone tomorrow. But I won't be searching so desperately any more. I know I must accept community where you offer it to me. I accept it in this moment. Thank you, Jesus.

We can't make it alone, Jesus

God knows, we've tried, and we've even reached the point where we could blow up everybody, including ourselves. Teach us how to listen carefully and patiently to other people. Teach us how to say what we have to say clearly, simply, and openly. Teach us what responsibility toward you and others really means.

Cut through all our egoism and self-interest, Jesus. Make us understand what patriotism must mean in one world of conflicting nationalisms. Educate us to support community wherever it brings people together in a shared sense of human concern. Work with us, Christ, to bridge gulfs and divisions between nations and persons.

What can I do about war and peace?

How can I do anything that will affect the power structures which hold the key to basic decisions about waging war or maintaining peace? I've marched in peace demonstrations, fasted in protest against nuclear experiments, signed petitions, and tried seriously to study the issues involved. But what have I been able to accomplish?

I know we can't pass over this situation, yet we are somehow supposed to live with the outrage of doing exactly that.

I see the beauty of your creation, and am grateful, but then I see in my mind's eye the very real possibility of its destruction. How can I stand this, Jesus? What is prayer supposed to mean if I am passively accepting a peril which it is sinful to accept? I don't want to misuse prayer to lull me about this crisis, Jesus. I want to accept my responsibility of cooperating with you in the continuing and present act of creation. How can I do that?

Three young children died in that room

It's just a room in a slum, in a big American city, but when a fire started it became a very special room, a death chamber for three youngsters.

They tell me eleven people have died in this area of a few blocks, Jesus. All died in fires when they were trapped and couldn't get out. The people in the area can't move away because there's no place for them to go.

It doesn't seem fair for some people to have nice homes with safety, Christ, while other people can't get out of a slum like this except in a coffin.

It takes away my guilt when I blame your murder on the Jews, Jesus

Why should I feel guilty about it? I wasn't there. If I had been, I can't imagine myself shouting anything about crucifying you.

The Roman soldiers were there, of course, along with Pontius Pilate. And the Jews were there, the Sanhedrin and those who cried for Barabbas instead of you.

I wasn't there, Jesus. I had nothing to do with it.

I *was* there, Jesus, as you know. I am a part of humanness, although I like to remember it only when I want something from my sister or brother or society at large, and like to forget it when it involves me in life outside myself.

I shouted for your crucifixion, Jesus. I taunted you as you bore your cross, and I stood in the crowd to watch you die.

I did this again just today, Jesus.

Forgive me. I ask for your mercy and forgiveness. But how can I ask forgiveness of Jews, after the pogroms, burnings, genocide, every form of discrimination, and most of it in your name? In your own humanity, you were a Jew. I am involved in your murder, Jesus, as in the lives and deaths of countless Jews. I ask forgiveness of you for the guilt I share in the deaths of Jews murdered by Christians in your name, for the guilt I share in the countless persecutions of Jews by Christians in your name.

I am shamed. I am mute.

I believe that terror is evil, Jesus

Sometimes I am tempted to use it when I angrily protest against the terrorism of the status quo. An eye for an eye. A tooth for a tooth. Injustice for injustice. A life for a life.

But if one became a tyrant to defeat a tyrant, wouldn't that already mean defeat? One would have become one's enemy, and corrupted.

Murder doesn't win people's hearts. Burning, exploding, and destroying don't make people love. "Love" is a misused word, isn't it, Jesus? Some people think it is soft to love. I don't think so. I believe that love can overcome hate. I believe that it can overcome terrorism. But why haven't we tried it?

My God, my God, why hast thou forsaken me?

We have conquered the moon and space. We shall vanquish foreigners who seek self-determination and move against our wishes or national policy. We shall defend the power of the status quo against black people, Latinos, Native American Indian people. Our future—is it written in plastic, in chrome, in dollars, in monumental waste, in guns, in nuclear overkill, in whiteness opposed to color, in respectability that breeds on personal salvation with indifference to the needs of others, in morality that is offended by the act of love but not the act of death?

My God, my God, why hast thou forsaken me?

The Nazi experience was only forty-five years ago. Organized religion accommodated the state and its own secure position within society. Severe repression lashed out angrily and mercilessly at dissent. The prophets? Let them be punished—tear out the tongues that offended! Burn the hands that wrote heresy against the state! Lash proud shoulders to wash them in blood! Silence the prophets. Silence them. Silence them.

My God, my God, why hast thou forsaken me?

We look ahead to the possibility of destroying life if we remain deadened to change, accept dumbly what is told us, and bury dissent and therefore freedom.

It is a time of self-examination, looking toward the conscience—and out to the world; seeking the focus of faith, the locus of love.

Meditations on Identity

✑ *She hadn't meant to let drugs take over her life*

At first it was just a thrill, a sensation; part of a longing for a sense of deeper awareness; fitting in as a part of her small circle of friends.

Soon, drugs became necessary—so she thought. The highs were brief, oh so brief, but demanding. The lows, unbearable, were when Irene scarcely functioned. It occurred to her: She *had* to get high again.

But she lost track of herself—who she was. Her marriage ended bitterly, her former husband taking custody of the kids. Her job—it was a great one, she had worked for years to get it and was ideally suited for it—disappeared amid embarrassment, despair, and guilt.

Friends drew away, for she began to move in an underside of life. Irene was obsessed, in thrall, destroying even the last vestige of what she perceived to be her true self.

Be with her in her treatment to get well, Christ. Guide her. Give her wisdom and strength for the struggle to live.

Masks

I. I was sitting on the subway coming into New York City. Did my face show the strange thing that had happened to me? These other faces, could they tell from my face the reunion I had had, after many years, linking who I am with who I was before? These faces, these masks, what had happened to them today? Maybe one of them had had a reunion, too, but masks are inscrutable.

If we do not have faces and cannot see each other, if this train simply goes on forever, could this be hell?

II. In museums I see masks that once served the purpose of opening up feeling, expressing emotion, revealing on the surface an inner fear or joy.

Yet, on the street or at a party, over lunch tables and office desks, I see masks that hide feelings and truth.

Sometimes one person needles and jabs at another until a mask falls to the ground, and a human face is seen in its nakedness and beauty. Even a pretty mask is somewhat grotesque and disquieting, so its absence is welcome.

It is absurd when two masks say to one another, "I love you." It is very touching when two human faces look lovingly upon one another.

✑ *A heavy frame separates me from the bearded man in the painting*

Does the frame provide him with an illusion of detachment or separation? I can see he's yawning.

Now he begins to come across as someone trying to play a smug role. He's certainly not succeeding, Jesus. I can see straight through his painted mask of nonchalance and exaggerated ease.

The man painted in oils inside the frame that separates us would like to communicate. So would I.

I want to throw away all frames, Jesus.

I'm a prisoner, Jesus

As you know, I built the jail with my own hands, stone upon stone, lock inside lock. Here I am a model prisoner of my own will, a slave of self.

My mind and body cry out for new life. My soul is parched, my life in decay, my dreams in shambles, my energy stifled. In this moment I am only sorry for myself, and feel hopeless.

Is there any use to struggle anymore? Oh, let me hear a cry of joy, see a burst of light. I'm tired of being a victim and a prisoner, especially of myself.

✑ *She's probably the most popular woman on the campus*

She's certainly one of the best looking, and she has a very real smile and seems completely secure, Jesus. You could hardly find anyone who dislikes her.

But she dislikes herself, or, at least, the self she feels she was handed but can't figure out. She thinks she must be two different selves, the operating one and another that is hidden under layers of complexity she can't get to. She wants to find out who that other self is because she believes she would like to be it. She simply doesn't know the self everybody seems to be relating to.

Everybody responds to her smile. She is tired of it and has come to feel it's a lie of some kind. She wants friends who would like that *other* self instead of this one which is a stranger—or enemy—to her.

The other night she broke up with the boy she likes. She cared too much about him to let him be hurt. She thought she should find out who she is before she lets anybody she cares about get too involved with *this* self. She wanted to love him with her other self, but didn't know how, or who that self might be.

Here she comes now, Jesus, smiling her way across the campus. Help me to smile back—at her *other* self.

Why can't we permit the liberation of people and living things, Jesus?

Why can't we permit our own liberation?

"The universe has consciousness," the young Chicano told me. "But the world is now uninhabitable. People are acting fiercely against the consciousness of the universe."

It seems to me we have a deadly definition of gods. We feel that to be a god is to ride roughshod over the earth, make decisions capriciously, act without feeling, and try to create terror in other people. We feel that to be a god is to claim the whole earth, and all of life within it, for our own use and destruction.

Could we start acting like humans, Jesus?

Meditations about Life and Death in a Retirement Home

“Go away”

she says almost inaudibly, forming the words precisely with her lips. Her eyes are hard.

I try to joke, play with her, soften this moment. It is part of my regular visit to her retirement home. Always in the past she held my hand, spoke to me earnestly with her eyes, entreated me not to leave.

Trying to affect a change in her depressed mood, I move my fingers in a playful way as if I were making dancing figures of them against a wall, talk to her and laugh.

“You’re crazy,” she announces, giving me an uncompromising look of dismissal. “Go away,” she repeats slowly. “Don’t come back.”

I feel frustrated and defeated; cannot imagine what has prompted her anger and rejection. A few moments later, a nurse speaks to me outside her room. “She’s feeling pretty low today. She’s always very unhappy when her daughter stays away a long time and doesn’t come to see her.”

Patience and understanding: they are needed especially in a retirement home.

∽ *"I want to die," she whispered*

That was during my last visit. Now the TV set is turned on loud, characters in a soap opera talk, and she doesn't see or hear them because she is asleep.

She's snoring, her head laid back on a pillow in the chair she occupies when she isn't confined to her bed.

She is over ninety years old. Loved by members of her family, she asked to be placed in a retirement home because she felt life would be easier for her here. Nonetheless, now she finds living itself an insuperable burden and would like to be released from any more of it.

Suddenly she awakens. She remembers an old prayer in German from her youth and starts to recite it. "A pillow," she whispers. "Please bring a pillow for my back." I talk to her for a while. She nods and smiles, occasionally utters a few words in German.

I kiss her forehead and say good-bye.

~ *She is still a beautiful woman in her eighties*

Always, she shows me what seems to be a genuinely motivated smile when she greets me. And she invariably wears a neat, good-looking dress and selected pieces of jewelry. A stylish hat sits next to her on her bed.

A photograph of her late husband is on her dresser. When she speaks of him, she cries softly. "I loved him so. I miss him. Why did he have to leave me alone?" But in a moment she has regained her composure.

On another visit, I find her holding a newspaper. "These poor homeless people on the street," she exclaims. "Isn't it awful?" Tears stream from her eyes, down her cheeks.

We say the Lord's Prayer together, and hold hands during it. She says the words firmly and loudly, her eyes opened, her head unbowed.

"It's good of you to come to visit me," she says, smiling. I see her as youthful, always getting ready to go out and confront life optimistically, expecting what is good and true to happen to her.

The fact that she could die so soon eluded me

On my recent visits I had noticed she was very frail, unsure, and her eyesight was failing rapidly. Yet her basic good humor was so intact, she fooled me.

The last time I saw her we were not alone. Her granddaughter, a college student, visited also. This provided an entirely different focus than usual for our conversation. There was a bright cheer to the occasion. Boisterous laughter replaced the sober note of previous visits when her problems were discussed, even though kept beneath a veneer of polite control.

So today I was unprepared, when I sought her out, to find she died last Tuesday. I suppose she died as she seemed to live: buoyant, smiling softly, taking simply another small step instead of a plunge.

I used to be afraid of her

Because she is totally blind and nearly deaf, she would jump when I drew close, reacting like a frightened bird. I didn't know how to calm her.

But then I learned simply to hold her two hands in one of mine, and place my other hand on her shoulder. This reassured her, provided her a necessary security.

"Who are you?" she asks me each time, in exactly the same voice. "I'm the man who comes to pray with you," I reply. "*Oh,* how *nice,*" she says, brightening.

We talk. She tells me sometimes that she used to give young students piano lessons. So, she explains, she is a very precise, disciplined person, one who wants to wrest exact meanings from words. After we say the Lord's Prayer, she explains that "thy will be done, in earth as it is in heaven" is much better than "on earth."

When I bring her Holy Communion, she asks "What is it?" "The bread of heaven," I reply. "*Oh,* how *nice,*" she says. Our ritual never varies. She accepts a sacramental wafer in her mouth.

Now her face lights. She holds my hands in one of hers, and with her other hand she traces the lines below my eyes, on my forehead. "The bread of heaven," she repeats quietly. We sit together without words, no longer afraid of each other.

"One of my sons just had his seventieth birthday," she says

She is ninety-five, delicate as a bird, yet an incredibly tough survivor. A while back she fell and broke her hip, but has recovered. Shingles come and go, visiting her face and head.

Her hair is neatly brushed this morning. She uses a cane when she gets up to open the door and greet me. She's wiry, energetic, agile.

Most remarkable, in my view, is how my visits to her ironically help *me*. Her sense of humor is strongly intact. Deeper than that, however, is a sturdy structure of faith, well-being, and an indestructible awareness of the continuity of life.

She is like an old tree whose roots penetrate into the earth. She has long weathered storms and years. Now she simply awaits the next season, whatever storm or peace may come.

Nonverbal Prayers

Daniel stands by the grave, wanting to pray, not knowing any words

He is forty years old, an intellectual and cultural figure in the city. Many years ago Daniel relinquished his religious background and community. He didn't look back and never felt a sense of loss.

Daniel married and became the father of a son eight years ago. The boy grew and thrived, and was a source of enormous joy and pride to Daniel. But a few days ago his son was killed in an automobile accident.

Daniel stands at the young boy's fresh grave. He feels a compelling impulse to *do* something besides just stand here. It occurs to him to say a simple prayer—perhaps for his son, or somehow about the entire situation surrounding his sudden and untimely death, with its resulting pain and confusion. Yet Daniel realizes he does not know the words of a single prayer.

His desire is to pray. His intention is to pray. Slowly, it dawns on him that he is expressing, "saying," incarnating a prayer, by being here.

Nancy is a teacher

Friends wonder why she's willing to work so hard for so little, to make this kind of a commitment in a world that often seems disinterested in unselfish giving.

Nancy sticks it out—the human and motivational problems she faces in the classroom, bureaucratic red-tape in the education system, the long distances she travels to work in a poverty area where she believes there is a special need.

How to teach students who are hungry and tired and disillusioned. How to interest them in ideas and challenges that may give them an opportunity to break out of an iron ring of deprivation and unequal opportunity.

Nancy stands at a blackboard, chalk in hand, talking and gesturing.

Our marching had a rhythm

About twenty of us had been marching in the snow, in a constant circular movement in front of an apartment house, for nearly three hours.

The time: 1961. The place: the inner-city of Detroit. We carried signs reading, "Negroes Can't Live Here," "We Oppose Discrimination," "End Segregated Housing," and "Freedom."

We marched because a black woman whom we knew had been denied housing in the apartment building because she was black.

It grew colder. Snow was falling quickly now, blanketing the sidewalk. The wind blew snow into our eyes. I removed my gloves and dug bare hands deep inside my overcoat pockets, flexing them to restore circulation. "Why can't people live where they want to?" a man angrily asked. That was, we felt, the point of our demonstration. People flashed glances from passing cars: quizzical, hating, noncommittal, friendly, bored.

Our picketing continued in the afternoons for four weeks until the black woman moved into the apartment house.

She has ten million dollars

Barbara won't be awake this morning when her maid arrives for work. In fact, the worst moment in her day is the first one upon awakening. She faces a gnawing emptiness.

It isn't that she has nothing to do. She is on a dozen symphony and art museum committees for big donors, and is a main contributor to a posh church that she attends without fail once each year on Easter morning. Daily she lunches at the country club or any restaurant of her choice. She can fly on an instant's notice to San Francisco, London, or Sydney.

Yet all the therapy in the world hasn't given her a motivating reason to face another day. A pragmatist, Barbara got off liquor a long time ago and resolutely stayed off it. Boredom is the enemy. Her husband walks through his own paces, which meet hers in the midst of yet another social gathering. Her children, away at school, are strangers who smile handsomely when they hold out their hands for more money.

God, she wishes that something mattered.

Joe is getting drunk again

He doesn't drink the hard stuff anymore, only beer and wine, but that's lethal brew for him. He's naked, seated at the kitchen table. And alone. Susan, his wife, left last week for what she said would be the last time.

Joe's driver's license had long permitted him simply to drive from home to work, and back. He violated that agreement many times, and ten days ago was the cause of a traffic accident. He has no license now. He was fired from his job for lousing it up, this following a period of probation which he broke by continuing to drink.

He has a six-pack on the floor and a gallon of cheap wine open on the kitchen table. Joe pours another tumbler of warm, sweet white wine.

His mind moves back over the years to a happy marriage, a good job, a promising career, friends too numerous to count on the fingers of both hands.

Right now, he is without any of these. There is nowhere to go, no phone calls to place, no hope of anything new in his life. Joe sits in the chair and looks at a blank wall. His open hands ask.

For nine years, Ken was a dialysis patient, kept alive by a kidney machine

"I've had hundreds of transfusions," he said. "I received four pints of blood every three weeks during that time. A shunt was put in my arm—a plastic hose attached to an artery and a vein deep in my arm."

When he had a mysterious bout with high blood pressure, the medical decision was made that a transplant was necessary. The wait began for a good kidney match. It was found. "What did all this mean? Would the transplant work? Who had died that I might live and have a better chance at life? I remember that things got hazy with shots, surgery lights and an unpleasant gadget in my throat."

The transplant was successful, but there was no certainty it might not be rejected after one month, one year, or five years of good functioning. "One of the things about having a terminal disease is that I find I can be intellectually honest and not play games," he explains.

Ken laughs easily and gently, greeting a doctor who has just come in to see how he is doing. Trying to go on living is an adventure.

Pam is a volunteer twice a week in a city shelter for homeless people

She also holds down a job and lives with her two young children, whose support she provides, and her mother. Pam discovers excitement in dozens of small challenges and events that make up her days. Hope, not a mere word for her, is translated into serving others.

After watching her grandmother slowly die in a county nursing home, Pam is grateful she can take care of her mother. She delights in her children, and thanks God she has strength to provide for their needs.

Pam rides to work on a bus. Today is nasty, drizzling and cold, outside the bus window through which she looks. But Pam is animated and happy. Riding the bus becomes another of her prayers in yet another day of fresh wonder. Pam's prayer is her work for others, her work for others prayer.

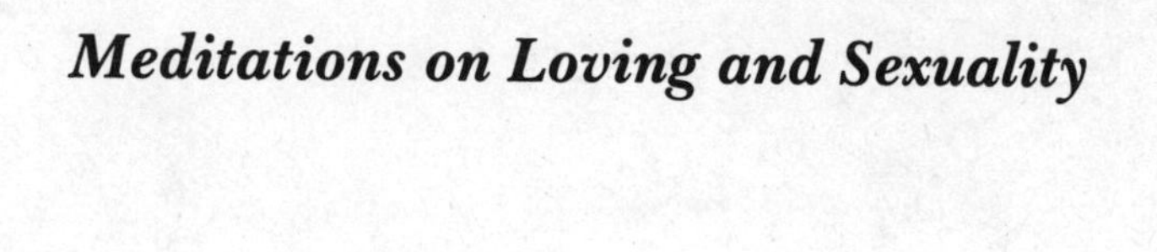

Meditations on Loving and Sexuality

~ *This young girl got pregnant, Christ,and she isn't married*

There was this guy, you see, and she had had a little too much to drink. It sounds so stupid, but the loneliness was real. Where were her parents in all this? It's hard to know. For the girl, they probably seemed indifferent, absorbed in their familiar routines, uninterested in her real life. But did she ever try to tell them about it? And would they have listened?

Now the guy doesn't want anything to do with her; he's tied up in some job and is very busy. He's especially annoyed about the idea of the child and wonders why she didn't know better. He thought she understood what the rules were: a woman doesn't have to get pregnant these days if she doesn't want to.

The girl is sitting across from me now, so cool and collected. She can't even admit to herself how hurt she is, and goes on analyzing the situation with bits of freshman psychology. And meanwhile there's a new life growing inside her, making new demands on her; does the textbook have an answer to that?

There's nothing ahead for her with the guy. She tells me he's really in love with somebody else. She's not in love with anyone; she's sure of that. And she's honest enough to admit, even knowing what she does now, that she'd go back to sleeping with the guy. Does she really think that's all she needs? She admits she's thought of suicide, but says she doesn't have the strength to make any real decision, let alone that one.

What am I going to tell her, Jesus? How can I help her understand the nature of the love she's looking for?

Ken and Tom stand before the altar in a church

They have decided to throw in their human lot together, to share and love each other—in sickness and health, prosperity and poverty, enthusiasm and despair.

Both had yearned for a shared life, creating a real home with friends, responsibilities, and interests in common. Each looked for another man with whom to share wholeness.

Ken's mother and father are here. Tom's parents, opposed to his being gay and to this service, are absent. A few of their siblings are here. The minister is giving a short homily following music and readings. Ken and Tom will exchange rings and say a few words to each other, expressing their love and what this covenant of commitment means to them.

They hold hands and are smiling.

You share my time and space, heart, my being

After we make love, you hold me in your arms. My heart pounding, I lay upon your chest. We stay here quietly. My universe is defined by the perimeter of your flesh, consciousness, and soul.

I think of getting up to make two cups of coffee. Shall we read the morning paper, get dressed, go out? But I don't move.

Bless us, Jesus. Bind us close. Let us have more days and years of joy, growth, responsibility, passion, quiet, and trust as your gift.

Each of them is afraid to start over with someone new, but they imprison each other

They are an attractive couple. They have a number of friends and go out a good deal socially. Marian and Larry share a double bed but have not engaged in sex for more than two years.

"This sex thing is ridiculous," she says, and goes on to insist she will visit her attorney on Monday morning to break up their marriage. But she doesn't.

Close to each other, they're far apart. It isn't only their sexual needs they cannot meet. They drink too much, have many brutal arguments. Yet they are grateful for kindnesses and connections, share a deep concern for each other's welfare.

What holds them together more than anything else is the fear of aloneness and a kind of pity. Each is afraid to start over with someone new. So, they're coasting on what they have, and losing themselves more and more in emptiness. Can they relinquish their escapes and turn to each other in a mutual confession of need, a new commitment to life?

They have been in love for forty years

They will be the first to say it wasn't all a bed of roses. They accepted their marriage as the most important fact in their lives, so they simply spent more time and energy on it than on anything else.

Of course, it meant not spending an excess of time and energy on each other. Instead they got involved, often separately, with a lot of other people and their concerns.

Humor has helped a lot. And the discipline of getting on with it in place of wondering whether they ought to or not. Listening as well as speaking. A healthy development of sexual fantasy to let sex remain exciting, not become routine. An unrelenting awareness of how stiflingly boring boredom can be.

They give love to life.

They've been married for twenty years, Jesus, and they say they hate each other

They want a divorce—that's the one thing they're sure of. Not that either of them is in love with anyone else. There just doesn't seem to be much love in the whole situation. Was it simply sex that brought them together, and sex that is killing them now?

They keep accusing each other of long-standing infidelities, and tell you they would have broken up long ago except for the children, but the children seem merely weapons to be used against each other. And then, when they've finally decided—once again—to make a real break, they end up in bed together at 4 A.M., and everything is fine until the next evening, when they feel it's time for a final break again.

They've hurt each other so terribly; no marriage counselor can undo what they've worked at so long. They've been to the psychiatrist and the minister and anyone else who would listen, with or without being paid for it, but no one knows how hate and love get so mixed up with each other. Or wasn't there any love here, Christ, ever?

Where do sex and love come together in these two lives? Should they try to make it alone or together? Can they make it together, Jesus? Can they make it alone?

She meets him at her apartment when he lies to his wife about why he's not home

What does she expect of this brief encounter? She experiences a searing, sweet, romantic sensation with a time limit. She expresses a naked, hungry need to pour out her unfulfilled life. Yet he has told her he is happily married and does not intend to leave his wife.

She wonders, more and more, what it means to "make love." The good-byes she has to say, and accept, are cool and brittle. She asks herself if the final one won't be a tersely bitten-off end that seems to jab like a needle seeking blood.

How much hurt can she stand? Will she come to understand what a full sexual union involves in terms of human relationship?

They are a couple in love, Jesus, but think they can't afford marriage yet

He is twenty-one, she is nineteen. They have been having sex for two years. Now he has found out that she hasn't been enjoying the sex but has been pretending to. "She feels guilty because we aren't married," the young man says. "What can we do? If we can't have a healthy sex life together, I'll call the whole thing off."

She accuses herself because she knows she went after him in the first place. She doesn't mention marriage to him, even though she would be more than happy to work to support him while he stayed in school. She even realizes that her very attitude of acceptance may be an unfair pressure on him.

Can they make something out of their situation? They're at least trying to talk to each other. The boy is smart enough to know that this problem is more than not having enough money, and is willing to admit that his pride has been hurt.

Take their mutual honesty, Jesus, and work with it.

~ *She is serene in the world and with her lover*

At first, her marriage to Christopher was a happy experience. Motherhood followed. They had three children together. After a long time the realization came that she was not fulfilled as Christopher's wife.

But why? There was no other man who attracted her. When she met Dorothy, the truth leapt at her irresistibly. Yet she found difficulty initially in accepting herself as a lesbian. Hadn't she known herself through all the previous years?

The love she felt for Dorothy was overwhelming and satisfying. It became the greatest challenge of her life to change her primary relationship with grace and a minimum of hurt and misunderstanding. Christopher was aware theirs had long been an unrewarding relationship, and he acceded to her wishes for a divorce. The children, out of college and into their own careers and relationships, understood.

She and Dorothy settled into their new life as partners and lovers, this at an age when many people turn away from risk. These two women are actively loving in a human, spiritual, and sexual relationship.

They ask for your blessing, Jesus.

Prayers for Racial Freedom

I see black and white, Jesus

I see white teeth in a black face.
I see black eyes in a white face.
Help us to see *persons,* Jesus—not a black person or a white person, a red person or a yellow person, but human persons.

How may the heart be taught, Jesus?

When a mind is closed and communication has ceased, how may a person be reached? If one's heart has never learned to love, or has stopped loving, how may the heart be taught, Jesus?

What happened to equal opportunity, Jesus?

It's a phrase used a lot twenty years ago. Blacks, Latinos, Asians, and other minorities were supposed to have a new deal that gave them an equal chance with white people to get ahead.

But Robert and Mary, who are black, don't see it around them or as a real possibility. They live in a section of the city that remains poor, rundown, and unequal in everything from education to city services. They raised their family here. Now they are threatened by warring youth gangs and drug dealers who are merchants of death, and their neighborhood is as dismal and alienated as hell. Poverty remains constant, with fear and taxes.

What can be done to make their lives equal, Jesus?

I find it very difficult to pray in this situation

It seems to me we all have prayed a long time about situations like this, yet have done little or nothing to change them. Maybe we thought prayer was magic, Jesus, and decided we didn't need to cooperate actively with you in working for a better world.

What are we to say about this family that lives in a wooden shack here on a winding dirt road? The father, a black laborer, earns less than a few thousand dollars a year under the modern slavery of "the plantation system." The mother is now bearing her seventh child. The family is hungry. As I see it, these persons have no opportunity to break out of the grinding, desperate life in which they have been prisoners since birth.

Lots of well-fed, comfortable, middle-class people everywhere are praying for "situations" like this all the time. But they don't seem to do enough about changing such situations by altering political and economic facts of life, or helping specific men, women, and children who are victims.

Isn't prayer expressed in action, Jesus, and isn't real action a form of prayer? Then maybe people in Chicago ought to pray for "situations" like this by getting involved in Chicago community organization efforts and in the lives of Chicago victims; perhaps people in Boston, London, São Paolo, and Johannesburg ought to pray in this way, too. And people in Mississippi, New York, Ohio, and Texas.

Otherwise, wouldn't it be more honest not to go through the mere motions of praying, Jesus? I mean, if we do not intend to offer ourselves and cooperate with you in fighting evil?

I feel so old when it comes to blacks and whites, Jesus

I can remember when blacks and whites could not eat together in a public dining room or stay at the same hotel. Looking now at the black students surrounding me, I realize this is a part of their folklore or past history, and not their present experience.

I recollect a visit I paid to a university in the South, Jesus, years ago. Whites and Negroes—as blacks were then called—were scattered through the dining hall at a luncheon in my honor. That is to say, people were not seated in rigid color blocs. This seemed healthy and promising. But most of the whites and blacks present had never laid eyes on each other before. Blacks were singularly unwelcome here. The atmosphere could have been cut with a very sharp knife. Nobody seemed to breathe normally.

When this reality finally got through to me, I tried to break the tension. I told a few of the extremely funny, warm, and earthy stories that had grown out of the civil-rights struggle. No one laughed, Jesus.

Inside that room, Christ, both the blacks and whites had been conditioned—for how long?—not to trust each other at all. They had been taught not to look at each other as human beings but only as "Negroes" and "whites."

Many people have died for the cause of racial freedom, Jesus. Will it be won?

"A White Man's Heaven Is a Black Man's Hell"

I heard this song many, many times when it was sung by young black nationalists during civil-rights demonstrations in the early sixties. Would today's black students sing it too?

Yes, I suppose so. At least they would think it. For their experience of human life has been hemmed in by white power. I imagine they dream of getting away, even just once, from white judgments, ways of doing things, and ingrained attitudes toward black people.

This must be why an occasional black professor is such a welcome change from a white one. And a black administrator, a black judge, a black journalist, a black TV personality, a black priest, or a black mayor.

"A white man's heaven." It would be hell in its isolation, wouldn't it, Jesus?

Juan lives in two worlds, Jesus

He is an undocumented Latino worker from Mexico. He paid four hundred dollars to get across the border. He works in a small Mexican restaurant, lives in a barrio, speaks only enough English to get by, sends money back each month to his wife and two kids in Mexico, and wonders what the future holds for him. He could be picked up by authorities and deported at any moment.

Juan feels hostility and misunderstanding from the black, Asian, and Anglo people all around him. He can't get a good job, make a home, and bring his family here, buy a car, or fit into a constantly changing new culture that baffles him in its diversity, indifference, and competitiveness. Sometimes he feels deep rage, other times a sense of depression that drains his energy.

He doesn't want to go back to grinding poverty and hopelessness, yet can't make any real sense out of life here.

Will Juan ever find out how to live in one world, Jesus?

They hate everything white

They're mad, Jesus, because they know they're black—and without authentic freedom, full civil rights, or economic equal opportunity. They have learned not to believe either white promises or white declarations about love and justice.

A black student said, "I refuse to be a textbook for whites. I don't want a white roommate in the dorm. On my own time, I need to study or be with friends to relax. I'm not going to teach a white kid with my life."

But a white student explained he didn't feel he should be made to pay for the sins or failures of his grandparents or parents.

Be with the black student and with the white student, Jesus, and help each to understand how the other feels. Where do all of us go from here—into one world or separate worlds? Tell us what you want us to do in specific situations, and how to do it. Time is running out, Christ.

They are called an interracial couple, Jesus

What is that supposed to mean? He is a man, she is a woman, they love each other and are married. He is black, she is white.

But the rest of us have a way of making life rather difficult for them. We are color-conscious, and so we stare at them. Some of us are racists, and so we hate them.

Their marriage is a good one. Their baby, who doesn't belong to either a white or a black ghetto, seems to have an excellent chance of being free in an emerging new society.

Are we going to let this couple be free by accepting them, not on color lines, but as a man and a woman who have become husband and wife?

It was a strange party, Jesus

The people seemed to be tense. They were in constant motion and playing tight roles. Everybody was scripted and choreographed.

I saw a white woman dressed in gold pajamas and enough costume jewelry to sink an excursion boat. She had had too much to drink. She kept saying, "I want to work with the poor in Africa . . . The poor . . . Africa . . . I want to work with the poor in Africa."

I wondered what she really wanted, and what was her Africa.

He doesn't know how his children are going to eat tonight, Jesus

There is just no money left. He has tried everything but cannot find a job. His wife is sick and doesn't have the right kind of care.

His little girl is crying. The sound of it is a bit louder than the dialogue of an old movie that is playing on the TV set. His boys are sitting huddled on an old sofa, watching the images flicker on the television screen.

Jesus, he wishes that he knew what to do.

⌯ *Black is not alien to me*

It used to be. It was different, so I feared it. White was supposed to be clean, pure, and holy. Black, I was taught, was its opposite. Was black a coal pit of sin and a moonless night of death?

I saw a black face. It smiled. I saw the Manichaean contrast of white teeth. I could not smile back. Who was this strange creature?

The first time I was alone as a white in a room filled with black men and women I was disturbed. I tried to breathe evenly. What was expected of me? I laughed, smiled, frowned, told jokes, sought emotional refuge.

Now I can discern black friendship, black anger, black hurt, black love, black deceit, black rage, and black tenderness. These are human and a part of me.

Black is not alien to me, Jesus.

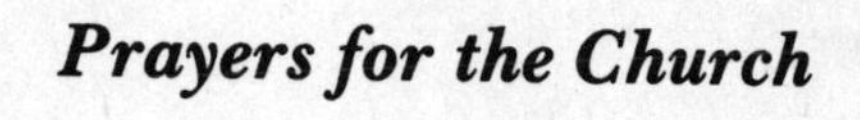

Prayers for the Church

A Dialogue Prayer by two seminary students, John and Carol, who have been preparing to enter the ministry

JOHN

I'm packed.
I'll be ready to go after chapel and breakfast in the morning.
It will be strange not to be here.
I'm a stranger to the man I was.
Carol and I entered the seminary together.
We were giving our lives to God.
What were we like three years ago?
Carol has changed as much as I have.
She's staying here.
It isn't simply staying or leaving that's important, but what's honest to do.
My life has never been so right as it is now.
There's the feeling of a clean line about it.
Tomorrow. Tomorrow morning I'll leave.

CAROL

My world, it's shaken to its foundations. John didn't know what conflict he started in my life when he decided to leave.
At first I thought I should go with him.
I've been critical of the same things.
I've felt the same futility and hopelessness.
Nothing *really* seems to change.
This, despite changes.
But afterward you look closely and see too few of them.
The reason I'm not going with John is that I still think there is hope working for change in the church from the inside.
I believe in the foundations and essential structure of the church.
In the long run, John may do more by leaving the seminary to preserve the essential structure of the church than I'll do by staying.
Only time will tell.

JOHN

I feel that I finally know who I am.
It isn't easy for me to leave the seminary. I've put my whole life into this.
Future directions are hazy for me. There's no easy road map to follow.
The alternatives are potentially cruel, but I'm no longer so afraid of cruelty.
I'm more afraid of dishonesty, especially in myself.
It's honest for Carol to stay.
It's honest for me to go.
If I have to suffer some hardships now, I say yes to them.
I acknowledge my needs as a person.
I can't think only about tomorrow.
I must be a whole man today.

CAROL

Yesterday. Today. Tomorrow.
How do these relate?
I respect the traditions of yesterday.
I want to live fully today.
I believe in the fulfillment of tomorrow.
Does this make me a conservative?
John places today ahead of yesterday and tomorrow.
Is John a radical?
I think I can be a whole woman working inside the system.
It doesn't threaten my existence.
John forced me to make a free choice.
Stay or leave. Like that.
I'll stay.

JOHN

After my first year in the seminary, I discovered that I knew *everything* about God.
He was omnipotent.
He was omnipresent.
He was omniscient.
He was *He*.
Onward, Christian Soldiers.

CAROL

They taught me never to be angry or lose my temper.
To love everybody, be available to all people at all times.
To be Christlike.
To pray more than other people.
Some of my teachers said the church was not involved in the sinful world, such as
  real estate
  ward politics
  racism
  war.
No.
  It was holy.

JOHN

Clergy will
conduct public worship
minister to the sick and dying
baptize babies
marry people
bury people.
Will clergy
  March on a picket line?
  Preach a disturbingly honest sermon?
  Knowingly lose money for the church by telling the truth?
  Protest actively against institutional racism?
  Stand publicly against war and warfare?
  Go to jail for religious convictions?
  Feel lonely?
  Fight inside the system to change the system?

CAROL

It was during our first year in the seminary.
John and I both felt totally inadequate to be here.
We felt sinful because we didn't love God enough.
We wanted the drives within us for ministry and a better world to become more holy.
John and I decided to pray together.
  On two nights a week we set our alarm clocks for 2 A.M.
  We met in the chapel.

We knelt down on the stone floor.
We prayed silently.
Body of Christ, save us.
Blood of Christ, inebriate us.
Passion of Christ, strengthen us.

JOHN

For an examination, we had to be able to list all the books of the Old Testament in order.
I stayed up all night, cramming.
Genesis, Exodus, Leviticus,
Numbers, Deuteronomy, Joshua,
Judges, Ruth, I Samuel. . .
Study the prophets.
But don't recognize one sitting in the room with you.
He or she might rock the boat.
He or she might upset the status quo.
Study church history, but don't make it.

CAROL

The difference a few people made.
The right time and the right place.
John XXIII
changed the church.
Shook up the Catholic world.
Shook up the Protestant world.
Bonhoeffer
forced me out of the religious ghetto into the whole world.
Religionless Christianity.
I'm glad I am living now.
I can stay in the system.
I can help change the system.
Dorothy Day
was an honest witness for truth
ran soup kitchens
fed the poor
prayed
fought for justice.

JOHN

The French worker-priests.
They wanted to be close to people.
They didn't want any separation between their lives and the real lives of ordinary people.
They wanted the church to stand with the poor, not the privileged against the poor.
The establishment tried to break them.
It failed, although the movement seemed to die or go underground when it was outlawed.
Unless a grain of wheat falls into the earth and dies, it remains alone; but if it dies, it bears much fruit.
I feel a close kinship to these worker-priests.
My interpretation of them is one reason I'm leaving.
I want to work as a Christian with people's secular concerns.
I don't want to spend my life and energy battling the establishment.
Can I bypass it and be a Christian in the world?

CAROL

Why was I born into *this* age?
Nothing can be the same as it was.
Old forms don't give new meaning to this generation.
I love old forms.
To worship before an ancient altar.
To wear bright vestments.
To hear the Eucharist sung very, very well.
I love these things.
I find them exhilarating and meaningful.
This doesn't mean God is only *here*.
It means, at its best, that God is here and therefore everywhere in the world.
But this is an age of pragmatism.
Mysticism must, it seems, be found in involvement in the world.
I shall stay in the church and try to build bridges to the world outside it.
John and I will have such a bridge.

JOHN

For I was hungry and you gave me no food.
I was thirsty and you gave me no drink.
I was a stranger and you did not welcome me.
Naked and you did not clothe me.
Sick and in prison and you did not visit me.
I'll try to be with Jesus in the world.
I'll end up working with people, without a collar or a portfolio.
Without the church's ordination.
I say yes to this.
As Jesus is in me, I'll be a priest, but hidden.
  Social action instead of organized religious activity.
  Prayer actions in the place of mere prayer words.
  Savior of life instead of the church.
  Liturgy as action in life, not actions in ritual.
I am whole.
  I want to be for God, in the midst of life.

CAROL

I am whole.
I'll be a juggler, like John.
Like John, I'll try to be a fool for Christ's sake.
There will never again be a neat, ordered pattern for me.
I can only try to follow Jesus' way of life.
I'll try to do this within the church and the world.
To see through the stained-glass windows.
To see Jesus in people's lives.
To see Jesus resurrected from religious forms as well as death.
To understand resurrection as freedom.
Not license.
Freedom.
I'll be busy.
  John, my brother, what *is* discipleship?
  We can try to find out and share it.

~ *An ordination prayer*

When you say to us "Go," and we comprehend our ministry in the world, do we understand that we will not be contenders in a social popularity contest? Do we perceive that all men and women, including ourselves, prefer to reject your Word rather than accept it? For to accept it means death to the old person and emergence of a new one in fire and love.

Do we realize that we are not to go forth into honor or social acceptance, prestige in the community, or increased wealth, even a comfortable status at home or an unchanged interior life?

Do we *want* you to call us with your command "Go"? Are we ready for this challenge? Or would we rather you did not call us? Then we could be left alone by you. We would not have to love in the face of hate. We would not have to proclaim your Word to people who will greatly resent it and largely reject it—and us. We could be individual islands in life, untouched by divine commandment and human need. Or could we?

Jesus, why do you call us when you know our sin, our failures, our inadequacy, our vanity, our absurdity, our weakness? When you call us, will you give us the strength to do what you ask?

Holy Communion

Jesus, we're here again. What are we doing here?

I mean, how is communion with you possible? You're holy, and we're very human. Yet I remember that you also became human.

I wonder how we can honestly be nourished and cleansed by your body and blood. Yet I realize communion is an outward and visible sign of an inward and spiritual grace. I accept this mystery.

We are grateful for this intimacy with you, Jesus. We thank you for letting us share this corporate action as we offer to God all of creation, including our own lives. Give us faith to understand what it means to be thankful.

Prayer for a baptism

Don't let this be simply a social occasion, Jesus. Touch the hearts of those present who associate Christianity only with superficiality and have become accustomed to religious exercises devoid of integrity or real meaning.

Someone is being baptized into your own life and death. Someone is being made a member of the church, your own body. Don't let this baptism be shunted off into a small corner of a big church, or into a quiet hour with a handful of people. Let this baptism be a principal part of the whole church's life, Jesus. Make us all realize that we are profoundly involved in it because someone is being ordained to a lifetime of discipleship and ministry in your spirit and name.

Grace at mealtime

Thank you for this food, Jesus, thank you. We're grateful that we can eat when we're hungry. We're also happy and grateful that we can do it together and not be alone, without each other or you.

Nourish our bodies and minds as well as our souls. Make us stronger, especially in our wills, so that we can serve you and others instead of just asking favors for ourselves.

Show us the real needs of others, Jesus. You told us that when we do anything to any of your brothers and sisters—and ours—in the world, we actually do it to you. When do we pass you by because we pass by one of your loved ones who is in need? Teach us to see your face, Jesus, when we look into our brothers' and sisters' faces.

Thank you for energy and strength, mercy and love.

Amen.

Invocation for a service organization

God:

First, we pray that this may not be merely a superficial outward form of prayer to which we give a respectable attention that we believe is socially proper, yet may actually ignore or even rebuke as a mere outward form drained of inner dynamic and honest, radical meaning.

Second, we offer thanks for the love ethic you have given us, and for all social justice, nonviolence, and peace, wherever these are found and particularly where they indicate active opposition to injustice and false peace.

Third, we ask for your judgment upon immoral systems that pervert the law to serve their own unjust ends, all totalitarian persecution, and any racial discrimination.

Have mercy upon us. Unite us in the common cause of social justice, in worship that is dynamically related to life, and in the upholding of moral law. Grant us tension in the midst of false peace, and grant us that peace which passes all understanding, in the midst of the struggle in which we are engaged on earth for the dignity of people.

Amen.

⌐ *To Christ at Christmas*

Why do we celebrate your birth but not your death?

Why do we call ourselves after your name but refuse to follow after your life?

I see your face, Jesus, in the face of a man with AIDS, whose life is made hell by insensitive, selfish people who do not care. I see your face, Jesus, in the face of a lonely woman in a crowded city. I see your face, Jesus, as loved and unloved in the faces of people who hate and persons who love.

Christmas is a great mystery to me. (The way we practice it, is it a mystery to you, too?)

Through the sham and simplicity, the cruelty and joy, the exploitation and adoration of it, I see your face. Bless us, *us, us,* your brothers and sisters, your disciples, the humanity you died on the cross to redeem.

Thank you, Christ, on the occasion of Christmas and always, for giving us life in the midst of death, *life, life,* with you.

A prayer of discipleship

"Send me."

But where? To do what?

To bring pardon where there had been injury in a life I casually brushed against at my daily work? (But I had thought of mediating a teenage gang war in Chicago!)

To help turn doubt into faith in a person with whom I live intimately in my circle of family or friends? (But I had thought of helping a tired drunk from skid row!)

"Send me." Send me next door, into the next room, to speak somehow to a human heart beating alongside mine. Send me to bear a note of dignity into a subhuman, hopeless situation. Send me to show forth joy in a moment and a place where there is otherwise no joy but only the will to die.

Send me to reflect your light in the darkness of futility, mere existence, and the horror of casual human cruelty. But give me your light, too, Jesus, in my own darkness and need.

Prayer of repentance

God:

Take fire and burn away our guilt and our lying hypocrisies.

Take water and wash away our brothers' and sisters' blood which we have caused to be shed.

Take hot sunlight and dry the tears of those we have hurt, and heal their wounded souls, minds, and bodies.

Take love and root it in our hearts, so that community may grow, transforming the dry desert of our prejudices and hatreds.

Take our imperfect prayers and purify them, so that we mean what we pray and are prepared to give ourselves to you along with our words.

◦ *Here I am in church again, Jesus*

I love it here, but, as you know, for some of the wrong reasons. I sometimes lose myself completely in the church service and forget the people outside whom you love. I sometimes withdraw far, far inside myself when I am inside church, but people looking at me can see only my pious expression and imagine I am loving you instead of myself.

Help us, who claim to be your special people. Don't let us feel privileged and selfish because you have called us to you. Teach us our responsibilities to you, and to all the people out there. Save us from the sin of loving religion instead of you.

Jesus Prayers

Why is reality about you so shocking to us, Jesus?

They've made the cross you hung on so pretty.

I know the real cross wasn't pretty at all. But I guess I understand why they want to make copies of it out of fine woods and even semiprecious stones, because *you* hung on it.

Yet doesn't this romanticize your death and give it a kind of gloss it didn't have? Your death was bloody and dirty and very real. Can't we face it that way, Jesus? And can't we face the fact that you were a real man, living a human life, as well as God?

Help us to understand, Jesus, your pain and your prayer

On the cross, when you asked why God had forsaken you, what did it really mean?

Were you reciting an old psalm or were you actually conscious of having been forgotten by God in a terribly painful and lost moment of time?

People have said this moment represented the depth of your agony on the cross, a spiritual crucifixion within the physical crucifixion. They have said your mental anguish was fused here with your bodily torture.

Yet you cried out to God. You never felt totally cut off from God. To me this has always seemed your deepest prayer.

Help me to know what you meant here, Christ.

Do you need me to act as your public relations person, Jesus?

I don't think you do. I may work in your service, but your success doesn't depend upon my success. You do not fail if I am not effective. This frees me from a terrible slavery to myself under the guise of succeeding for you.

You are not mocked. Your reign has already come. It is established in human life. I can cooperate with it, but never usher it in.

Why do some people say it is necessary to win money, large numbers of converts, publicity, and prestige for you? It has led to the church's fatal silence on issues where following you would have meant its own loss of these things.

Some Christians speak of the church as an army. You are presumably the general, Jesus, and the army is supposed to fight valiantly for your victory in the world, even if it must sometimes kill, maim, or pillage.

Is anyone, anywhere, ever meant to be manipulated, sacrificed, or dehumanized for your success, Jesus?

☞ *Help us really to dig in, Jesus, and be with you*

After all the poor fiction and cheap biblical movies that have turned your life and death into almost bizarre superstition, Jesus, it's hard for me to see your cross as it really was.

They've even turned Jerusalem into such a tourist attraction that it's not at all easy, even while walking along the actual ground you walked, to visualize anything with honesty or accuracy.

I imagine it was sweaty and hot. When you said from the cross, "I thirst," I am sure you were very thirsty. It's easy for us today to say you were really thirsting for people's souls (and I'm sure you were), but isn't this just a dodge that keeps us from accepting the fact of your humanity? Why do we want to forget that you were a man, hanging on the cross for hours, who simply needed something to drink?

Can we somehow get through all the decoration that has been developed about the cross and just be quiet and be there with you?

Thanks for what you did about success and failure

Jesus, you ruined all the phony success stories forever when you didn't come down from the cross, turn your crown of thorns into solid gold, transform the crowd at Golgotha into a mighty army, march on Rome, and become *the king.*

Now every success symbol looks so shoddy and short-lived when it is placed against your cross. You accepted and overcame death. You showed us the dimension of life in God's eternal dispensation that makes the careers we plan and the standards we accept look absurd.

When you refused to play the role of a Great Man, or the ultimate Big Shot, you really made us level with your as yourself, Jesus.

Teach us the path, show us the way

They say that everyone has a cross to bear, Jesus. And you once said, "Take up your cross and follow me." What do these things mean? I think they mean that every person ultimately has to face up to reality—face one's own calling, destiny, nature, and responsibilities.

In your own life, Jesus, you faced reality directly and unequivocally. You incarnated the truth as you believed it. You didn't pander to any easy or obvious popularity. You attacked the hypocrisies of the human power structure head on. You rejected the status quo in favor of obedience to the Realm of God. And when it came to taking the consequences, you didn't shy away from torture and execution.

The way of the cross was your understanding of your mission and your faithfulness to it.

The way of the cross seems to be, for every individual Christian, the reality that dictates style of life, defines mission, and brings a person into communion with you.

Help me bear my cross on the way of the cross, Jesus.

~ *What is love, Jesus?*

It seems so important, Jesus, that you called on God to forgive your torturers because, as you put it, they didn't know what they were doing.

You kept on loving, even then.

Help us to learn from you, Jesus, how to keep on loving when we feel like hating. It's hard. Some of us have even turned your cross into a symbol of hate. When the Ku Klux Klan burns a cross, Christ, the blasphemy of it startles me. Doesn't this mean, in a very real sense, joining the ranks of your own executioners?

Nevertheless, you were actively, creatively, responsibly *loving*, even on the cross, Jesus. Help us to see that love for what it is—in all its fierce passion and sweep of forgiveness.

~ *Jesus, hold in your loving arms your brothers and sisters who have AIDS*

We badly need you to stand with us as we face AIDS, Jesus. It strikes brutally and shows no mercy. Our friends and loved ones are afflicted by it and many are dying.

Suffering with AIDS is like your own hanging on the cross, isn't it, Jesus? You know the searing pain that will not go away. You cried out from the depths of your human experience to ask if God had forsaken you.

You have completely shared with us the gut feeling of desperate fear and anguish. And you died before our very eyes, revealing unconditional love. When you rose from death, you shared Easter with us.

Yet please understand we're hurting so much in this moment that it seems nearly unbearable. We need the fullness of your love *now.* We need your hope running over *now.* We need the exuberance of your joy *now.*

Pour into us healing power to transform AIDS and stop it. Let the sweeping passion of your love be with us to confront the rage, pain, and loss.

Finally, give us the quiet serenity of your love to guide us into eternal life.

~ *It is dawn at the beach, Jesus*

A silver full moon keeps disappearing behind early morning clouds. Do I hear the heartbeat of the world as I listen to the sound of the ocean? Standing alone at the ocean's edge, I feel the awe and power of creation.

The wind blows an empty paper bag against my leg. The brown paper appears animated, assumes guises and shapes. The smell of the sea makes me conscious of the deep; out of the deep I have called to you.

The interior of no cathedral on earth can match this staggering immensity. Perhaps its sense of holiness can be found inside a great forest or on a desert beneath the stars.

Solitary, I am not lonely. I believe the whole universe shares its life with me; I am connected to it. Here, in this moment, Jesus, I want nothing. My strong awareness is gratitude for life. I am simply thankful.

There are fresh footsteps in the sand. Someone else has been here before me this morning. Is it you?

Are you running with me, Jesus?